Your Wealth in God's World

Does the Bible Support the Free Market?

John Jefferson Davis

Presbyterian and Reformed Publishing Company
Phillipsburg, New Jersey

Printed in the United States of America

Library of Congress Cataloging in Publication Data

Davis, John Jefferson.
    Your Wealth in God's World.

    Bibliography: p.
    1. Economics in the Bible. I. Title.
BS670.D28   1984   261.8'5   83-19286
ISBN: 0-87552-219-X (pbk.)

To Scott and Kimberly

Contents

Preface

There are many diverse opinions today on what the Bible teaches about wealth, poverty, and the role of government in our nation's economic life. In this small volume I have tried to present a biblically based position that avoids the dangers both of the "health and wealth gospel" and of excessive state intervention in our society's economic life.

My hope is that this volume will prove profitable to the evangelical community, particularly for study groups, college and seminary reading assignments, and individual use.

I wish to thank Carrie Powell, who so ably typed the manuscript, and Scott and Kimberly Hahn, whose friendship has been so valuable in formulating the perspective presented in this book.

John Jefferson Davis
South Hamilton, Massachusetts
1983

1

Wealth, Poverty, and Work:
The Biblical Roots

From Bloomingdale's to Benares

Imagine taking a fast jet from Bloomingdale's in New York City to Benares, India. In Bloomingdale's you see the incredible profusion of merchandise produced by the American economy: the latest designer jeans, the most fashionable cosmetics, gold and silver jewelry, watches, the newest electronic games and home computers, fashions by Calvin Klein and Pierre Cardin, sterling silver flatware, mink coats, leather boots, and much more.

The scene is different in Benares, a holy city of India on the Ganges River. Here you see public buildings in various stages of dilapidation. Moisture and heat have left pockmarks in the brick, stone, and plaster, giving the façades an appearance of dissolution and decay. Tailors squat and sew in crowded streetside workshops. Buffaloes covered with mud amble toward the river. Emaciated men and women sit begging in the dirty streets. Donkeys move slowly under their heavy burdens. A woman in rags pulls two dead rats on a string.[1]

All of America is not Bloomingdale's, of course, and all of India is not Benares. Nevertheless, our imaginary journey across vast distances in space illustrates, even more importantly, the vast distances between cultures and systems of belief. The enormous differ-

1

ences in wealth and material well-being are not accidental. They reflect fundamental contrasts between what the philosophers call "world views": our basic convictions about the nature of the world, human life, work, and wealth.

Why are some cultures wealthy and others poor? What is the Christian's responsibility in a world plagued with poverty and hunger? Does the Bible favor one economic system over the other? How should the government be involved in alleviating poverty? What do biblical principles of stewardship demand of the Christian in the latter part of the twentieth century? What does the Bible say about our system of free enterprise?

These are some of the issues we will face as we seek to understand our economic responsibilities in a complex world by means of the principles and commandments of biblical revelation. We will begin by seeing how basic economic principles are rooted in the biblical understanding of creation, human nature, divine providence, sin, Jesus Christ, and the Christian life.

Behold, It Was Very Good: the Doctrine of Creation

The book of Genesis tells us that when God had completed his work of creation, he looked upon what he had made and pronounced it "very good" (Gen. 1:31). Living in a culture influenced for two thousand years by the teachings of the Bible, we take for granted that the material world is neither evil nor unreal. But many other cultures would not share our view, as, for example, we saw in our imaginary trip to Benares. Our Western drive to develop our natural resources, to improve our material circumstances, and to take charge of our economic destiny reflects the basic conviction, rooted in Genesis, that life in this world can be a good and productive endeavor.

Because God's creation is good, there is no need to flee the world and seek salvation in heroic acts of asceticism. In the early church Simeon Stylites, a Syrian hermit, fled the world by spending the last thirty years of his life, until A.D. 459, perched atop a pillar east of the city of Antioch. Simeon's devotion to the cause of Christ as he understood it was remarkable, but we need not follow his understanding of Christian discipleship. Secular work and the possession of wealth are not contrary to true spirituality when used according to God's commands. They can express the goodness of the world God has made, and the Christian gratefully receives those good gifts as coming from the hands of the Creator. As John Calvin, the great Protestant Reformer, observed in one of his New Testament commentaries, "God . . . by ingrafting us into his Son, constitutes us anew to be lords of the world, that we may lawfully use as our own all the wealth with which He supplies us."[2]

The biblical understanding of creation lent heavily to the intellectual foundations of modern science and technology, without which the remarkable economic development of the West cannot be explained. There is a reason that modern science arose not in India or China, but in the Christian West. As the philosopher and historian of ideas Alfred North Whitehead has pointed out, the intellectual basis for modern science could not have been laid apart from the biblical teachings of a rational God and a good creation.[3] Eastern religions gave man little incentive to study the material world. The pioneering scientists of the seventeenth century, however, believed that because the universe was the handiwork of a wise and rational God, it was worthy of study, with patterns, design, and scientific laws there to be discovered.

Many of the early scientists understood their work as "thinking God's thoughts after him." In letters of 1613 and 1615 Galileo wrote, "Nor does God less admirably discover himself to us in Nature's action than in the Scripture's sacred dictions."[4] At the end of the second edition of his great work *Principia*, which laid the groundwork for the modern understanding of the laws of gravity, Isaac Newton declared, "This most beautiful system of the sun, planets and comets, could only proceed from the counsel and dominion of an intelligent and powerful Being."[5] These pioneering scientists could happily have sung the words of the popular Christian chorus, "In the stars His handiwork I see." Modern Western economies reflect the amazing productivity made possible by modern science, and modern science reflects the truth of the biblical doctrine of creation.

The goodness and glory of God's creation is also the basis for Christian stewardship of the environment. The psalmist could say, "The heavens are telling the glory of God, and the firmament proclaims his handiwork" (Ps. 19:1). As Gerard Manley Hopkins, a Christian poet of the last century, put it, "The world is charged with the grandeur of God."[6] As God opens our eyes to appreciate the beauty of his handiwork in nature, we find in ourselves an increasing desire not only to enjoy and develop the creation, but also to preserve it for future generations. The beauty of the world so sensitively portrayed by a Sierra Club poster is the Christian's heritage— to be enjoyed, and also to be managed responsibly by God's stewards in the world.

Made in the Image of God: the Doctrine of Man

The family is at the new mother's bedside in the hospital's maternity wing. The new baby, wrapped in a soft blue blanket, slowly opens his eyes and then gives a loud cry. "Why, he's the spitting image of his father," someone says.

We naturally look for resemblances between a newborn child and the parents. The Bible tells us that such a "family likeness" exists between God and his children, because we are made in the image and likeness of God (Gen. 1:26, 27). Of all God's creatures, we human beings alone have the spiritual, moral, and intellectual qualities designed for a personal relationship with God.

This biblical teaching of men and women as the image-bearers of God helps us to understand some basic features of economic life. Adam was given the task of naming the animals God had made (Gen. 2:19). Because Adam was made in the divine image, he shared in a derivative way God's own creativity and powers of imagination. This God-given ability to create and to see new possibilities for products, services, and labor-saving devices lies at the very heart of a strong and growing economy. Economic productivity that can produce a better quality of life for all is not just a matter of discovering new deposits of iron, coal, oil, and other physical resources, but is primarily a matter of new ideas, new insights, new leaps of the human imagination. As George Gilder, a best-selling economics writer, has put it, "Our greatest and only resource is the miracle of human creativity in a relation of openness to the divine."[7] One might conceivably train chimpanzees to sort apples and oranges, but only men and women made in the divine image and sharing in God's creative powers can design new computers, discover a new wonder drug, invent new medical applications for fiber optics, or send a man to the moon and back.

The biblical teaching concerning God's image also is what accounts for human individuality and diversity. While we are all made in the image and likeness of God, not one of us is a carbon copy of the other. Even identical twins have distinctive personalities, interests, and temperaments. God's power and creativity are so great that he can create billions of human beings without once repeating himself. Such human diversity is the basis for what economists call the *division of labor*. Both the plumber and the accountant benefit if the plumber can depend on the accountant to keep his books and the accountant can depend on the plumber to repair his pipes. The diversity of human interests, skills, and training allows each of us to concentrate on doing what he does best, and the whole society can benefit by countless such free exchanges.

Human diversity can be, through free exchange and division of labor, the source of a richer life for all. As the great Austrian economist Ludwig von Mises observed, "If the earth's surface were such that the physical conditions of production were the same at every point and if one man were equal to all other men . . . men would not have embarked upon the division of labor."[8] The same principles hold true for nations. If one nation is better at producing computers and another better at growing coffee, both nations will benefit if they concentrate on doing what they do best and then trade with one another.

When God made man in his own image, he gave the human race a "cultural mandate" to subdue the earth and to exercise dominion over the creation (Gen. 1:26-28). Men and women were designed not merely to react passively to the world around them, but to actively shape their environment. The urge to build and furnish a home, to establish a new business, to bring new roads, schools and industries into being is no mere accident of biology. It reflects the God-given urge to manage and develop God's world as his stewards. Animals merely live in their environment, but persons made in the image of God exercise dominion and create cultures and civilizations. Business activity is an outworking of this cultural mandate and, like everything else, is to be done to the glory of God (I Cor. 10:31).

God Is Working Out His Purpose: The Doctrine of Providence

"God is working his purpose out as year succeeds to year," read the words of the familiar hymn. These words express the biblical truth known as the doctrine of providence. Even though the Bible never uses the word "providence," the truth that God controls all that happens and guides all of history toward its appointed goal is taught in countless ways from Genesis to Revelation. Not even the tiniest sparrow falls to the ground apart from the will of the Father (Matt. 10:29). God overruled the evil designs of Joseph's brothers so that many people would be preserved from famine (Gen. 50:20). The sovereign God accomplishes all things according to the counsel of his will (Eph. 1:11).

The economic fortunes of Israel illustrate the doctrine of God's providence. Moses warns the people that if they break the covenant and disobey God's commands, God will remove his hand of blessing from their economic life: "If you will not obey the voice of the Lord your God . . . cursed shall be the fruit of your body, and the fruit of your ground, the increase of your cattle, and the young of your flock. . . . The Lord will make the rain of your land powder and dust. . . . you shall build a house, and you shall not dwell in it; you shall plant a vineyard, and you shall not use the fruit of it" (Deut. 28:15, 18, 24, 30). The prophet Haggai reminds the people that their economic troubles are not accidental, but have been sent by God to teach them that their spiritual priorities are out of order. God has sent inflation upon the land: "He who earns wages earns wages to put them in a bag with holes. . . . You have looked for much, and it came to little; and when you brought it home, I blew it away" (Hag. 1:6,9). What caused their problem? They were neglecting the work of rebuilding God's temple and busying themselves with building and furnishing their own homes (Hag. 1:9). The Bible makes it clear that spirituality and economic life are related. God controls both and uses economic events to teach his people spiritual truths.

Just as God providentially works through the laws of nature by which he has ordered the physical universe, so he also has established laws and principles for our social and economic life. The law of supply and demand, for example, was not invented by economists. This law, reflected in the production, distribution, pricing, and consumption of the vast array of goods and services available to American consumers, is rooted in our God-given human nature: our ability to make rational calculations; our desire to transcend our environment and to improve our circumstances; our diversity of tastes, values, abilities, and skills. What Adam Smith called the "invisible hand" is God's providential structuring of our economic and social life. Given the diversity of human tastes and abilities, if there is a sufficient demand for hot tubs or caviar or designer jeans or down jackets, there will be sufficient incentives for suppliers to market those goods at a price agreeable to both buyer and seller. Governments and nations that ignore the law of supply and demand inevitably produce inefficiencies, shortages, and black markets, as the experience of Iron Curtain countries, such as Poland, so vividly demonstrates. God has ordained basic economic principles just as surely as he has ordained the law of gravity, and we ignore such principles only at our own peril.

Far as the Curse Is Found: The Doctrine of Sin

"Far as the curse is found / far as / far as / the curse is found." I can remember puzzling as a young boy over these words from the Christmas hymn, "Joy to the World." At the time, I thought people were singing, *"For* as the curse is found." Not until after I accepted Christ during my senior year in college did I understand that these words, based on the third chapter of Genesis, refer to the consequences of the fall of Adam and original sin. And only much later did I realize that the biblical teaching about sin had important ramifications for economics, work, and the role of government.

Sin has a powerful effect not only on individuals, but on human institutions and activities as well. Adam was told that because of his sin, the very ground—the source of his livelihood—would be cursed, bearing thorns and thistles (Gen. 3:17, 18). From then on man would earn his bread by the sweat of his brow (3:19). Because of the disobedience of our first parents, we all are subject to death and enter the world with a sinful nature (Rom. 5:18; Ps. 51:5; Eph. 2:3).

The consequences of the fall and original sin are many. Because the whole creation has been subjected to futility and decay (Rom. 8:20, 21), things are not the way they should be and have a built-in tendency to "run down" and degenerate. In a fallen world, a child, through no fault of his or her own, can be born with a serious congenital defect (cf. John 9:1-3, the man born blind). No matter whether our work is in the home, the office, the field, or the factory, there will always be disagreeable and burdensome elements involved in it. Significant social and economic reforms are possible and desirable, but in an imperfect world, the poor will always be with us (Matt. 26:11). Because of the reality of sin, we as Christians know that all institutions—whether government, business corporations, labor unions, universities, or the media—are flawed and can never in and of themselves bring society to some state of utopian perfection. Only Jesus Christ—not human effort, organizations, or wisdom—can bring in the kingdom.

One of the most important consequences of sin for our understanding of economics and the role of government relates to the danger of concentrating power in the hands of too few people. Sinful men and women inevitably are tempted to abuse power. When the people of Israel asked for a king so that they could "be like all the nations," Samuel warned that the king would build a large bureaucracy to serve him, conscript their sons and daughters for his service, and lay heavy tax burdens on them (I Sam. 8). The history of the kingships in Judah and Israel shows that Samuel's warnings were correct.

Lord Acton, the British historian, once observed that "power corrupts, and absolute power corrupts absolutely."[9] Our Founding Fathers knew this and were very careful to write into our Constitution checks and balances intended to prevent excessive concentrations of power. "The accumulation of all powers . . . in the same hands," wrote James Madison, the chief architect of the U.S. Constitution, "may justly be pronounced the very definition of tyranny."[10] James Madison had been a student of John Witherspoon of Princeton, the only clergyman to sign the Declaration of Independence. With Witherspoon, the future President had studied Greek, Hebrew, Bible, and Christian doctrine. Being well acquainted with the biblical teaching on original sin, it was no accident that Madison understood the need to build checks and balances into the Constitution.

Because of an understanding of human nature influenced by the teaching of the Bible, the Founding Fathers were committed to a philosophy of limited government. "What is government itself," asked the author of Federalist Paper No. 50, "but the greatest of all reflections on human nature?" The writer (either Hamilton or Madison) went on to observe, "In framing a government . . . the great difficulty lies in this: you must first enable the Government to control the governed; and in the next place oblige it to control itself."[11] The dramatic expansion of government power in the twentieth century demonstrates the difficulty of achieving that latter goal.

In framing the "establishment" and "free exercise" clauses of the First Amendment, which state that "Congress shall make no law respecting an establishment of religion, or prohibiting the free exercise thereof," the Founding Fathers safeguarded religious freedom by limiting the power of the federal government to involve itself in the affairs of the church. Given the dramatic growth of government in the economic sector of American life, some have suggested that today we need an "Economic Bill of Rights" to limit governmental interference in the economic freedoms of citizens. One of the greatest virtues of a free market economy in a democratic society is the dispersion of political and economic power into many hands. Socialist countries like the Soviet Union and the People's Republic of China, on the other hand, are like large "company stores" where both political *and* economic power are concentrated in the hands of the government elite. Such concentrations of power, whether abroad or at home, warned Madison, are the "very definition of tyranny."

In the Form of a Servant: Christ and the Christian Life

Albert Schweitzer, a world-renowned theologian and accomplished concert organist, captured the world's imagination when he resigned his university post to establish a hospital for impoverished Africans on the forested banks of the Ogowe River in French Equatorial Africa. By 1963, two years before Schweitzer's death, 350 patients were being served at his hospital, financed with Schweitzer's own personal income and outside gifts.

The spirit of self-giving service typified so dramatically by the life of Albert Schweitzer recalls the words of the apostle Paul in Philippians 2: Christ Jesus, though he existed with the very splendor and privileges of God, humbled himself and took on the form of a servant. His humility and obedience were crowned later by exaltation (Phil. 2:6-9).

That biblical pattern of humble service and subsequent reward lies at the heart of the free enterprise system at its best. In a free market economy, large rewards await those who consistently and imaginatively meet the needs of other people. As George Gilder has put it, "Capitalism . . . is capable of fulfilling human needs because it is founded on giving which depends on sensitivity to the needs of others."[12]

At the age of 42 William Nickerson retired from his telephone company job to devote full time to supervising the real estate activity he had started on the side. Nickerson, author of the best-selling book, *How I Turned 1,000 Dollars into a Million in Real Estate*, bought and rehabilitated a series of run-down rental units. He was richly rewarded for his efforts, which helped to provide living space for hundreds of people. He imaginatively saw an opportunity to serve human needs where others saw only dilapidated buildings, and as a result he reaped rich dividends.

The life of Christ and the teaching of the New Testament have influenced our modern Western view of work, in terms of both its dignity and its obligation. Jesus Christ, who stooped to wash his disciples' feet, and who himself was a carpenter, gave dignity to both manual labor and the service occupations. His example in the service of footwashing startled his disciples and formed a striking contrast to prevalent Roman and Greek attitudes, which considered such menial tasks and most manual labor to be fit only for slaves. Christ showed that even the most humble employment can become a form of service to God. "Whatever you do, do all to the glory of God" (I Cor. 10:31). Christianity gives spiritual meaning to the world of work.

The apostle Paul taught new converts in Thessalonica that diligence in work was a Christian obligation. Christians are not to live idle and unproductive lives: "If anyone will not work, let him not eat" (II Thess. 3:10). And as the seventeenth-century Puritan pastor Richard Baxter put it, "God has commanded you . . . to labor for your daily bread and not to live as drones off the sweat of others."

Not long ago Barbara Palmer, an investigative reporter for the *Washington Monthly*, discovered the following line item in a contract negotiated by the American Federation of Government Employees with the U.S. Department of Labor: "Employees have the right to play radios, cassettes, etc. on the worksite so long as the use does not disturb the productivity of the employee . . . and does not distract clientele." A bit of checking revealed that the "etc." referred to televisions. In other words, Labor Department employees claimed a contractual right to watch television while being paid to administer wage-and-hour laws and federal occupational safety regulations. "A lot of clerical people are into soap opera," one employee remarked.[13]

"Let the thief no longer steal, but rather let him labor . . . that he may be able to give to those in need," Paul taught (Eph. 4:28). This New Testament virtue of diligence in work helped to undergird the economic development of the West. That same biblical virtue must be cultivated anew if the American economy is to remain competitive during our time.

2

Obedience, Blessing, and Responsibility: Wealth and Riches in Biblical Teaching

The Christian looking for biblical insight on wealth and riches will encounter a confusing array of views in today's religious periodicals, books, and Christian radio and TV programing. "The New Testament condemns not just improper attitudes toward wealth, but also the mere possession of undistributed wealth," declares one biblical expositor.[1] Another well-known Bible teacher asserts that God *wills* the financial prosperity of every one of his children, and that for a Christian to be living in poverty is to be living "a Satan-defeated life." Preachers such as Brother Al and Reverend Ike tell their followers, "Serve God and get rich." Such conflicting claims raise the question, Are all these people reading the same Bible?

What does the Bible really teach? Is there a change from the Old to the New Testament in the biblical outlook on wealth? Is the mere possession of more than the bare necessities of life condemned by the Bible. Should American Christians feel guilty about their material abundance in a world where countless people are poor and hungry? Does God want every believer to be rich? Such questions call for an overview of the biblical teaching.

Obedience and Blessing: Wealth in the Old Testament

"The earth is the Lord's and the fulness thereof." This affirmation from Psalm 24 sets the tone for a biblical attitude toward wealth. All things belong to God, the sovereign Creator and disposer of all that exists. God's children are blessed with the riches of creation, but in the last analysis, we are but the managers or stewards—not the outright owners—of what God has, for a time, entrusted into our hands. Not only in tithing, but in all of life we are held accountable for our stewardship.

The God who graciously gave Israel an inheritance in the Promised Land also blessed individuals with wealth. Notable in this regard were the patriarchs Abraham, Isaac, and Jacob. Abraham was very rich in cattle, silver, and gold, and had great possessions (Gen. 13:2, 6). His son Isaac likewise became very wealthy, with flocks and herds and a great household, so that the Philistines envied him (Gen. 26:12-14). God's faithfulness to his covenant promises was demonstrated in the material blessings enjoyed by Jacob as well (Gen. 28:13-15; 32:10). Solomon and Job also enjoyed great material wealth (I Kings 3:13; Job 1:3; 42:10).

Obviously, not every Israelite was wealthy. For various reasons some were in fact poor. Nevertheless, in the light of these prominent examples from Old Testament history, it would be difficult to maintain that the mere possession of surplus wealth was sinful in God's sight. For the patriarchs, wealth was a significant element of God's covenant blessing.

The book of Deuteronomy contains some of the Old Testament's most important teachings on temporal prosperity. Moses warns the people that they will be tempted to forget God when they have entered the Promised Land, and when their gold and silver and flocks and herds begin to multiply. Prosperity will bring temptations of pride: "Beware lest you say in your heart, 'My power and the strength of my own hand have obtained this wealth.' Remember that it is the Lord your God who gives you the power to obtain wealth, in order to confirm the covenant which he made with your forefathers" (8:17, 18). Moses could foresee all too clearly the very human tendency to focus on the gift and to forget the giver.

Many centuries later, John Wesley lamented the tendency of English converts to "fall away from their first love" after they had become prosperous: "Wherever riches have increased the essence of religion has decreased in the same proportion. . . . as riches increase, so will pride, anger, and love of the world in all its branches."[2] No doubt there were notable exceptions, but Wesley's general experience seemed to confirm his stated observations.

The twenty-eighth chapter of Deuteronomy, one of the crucial passages in the Bible dealing with temporal prosperity, draws a clear connection between Israel's obedience to God's laws and God's blessing on that nation. If Israel is obedient, the nation will be blessed in agriculture, in family life, in trade, and in military engagements. If Israel is careful to heed the voice of God, then the Lord "will open to you his good treasury, the heavens, to give the rain of your land in its season and to bless all the work of your hands; and you shall lend to many nations, but you shall not borrow." The exact opposite will inevitably follow if Israel disobeys the laws of God: temporal curses instead of blessing, economic ruin instead of prosperity. As the commentator Matthew Henry once put it, "If they would not be ruled by the commands of God, they should certainly be ruined by his curse."[3] God was teaching that religion and economics are not separate parts of life, but are bound together in one plan and purpose of God, who controls history and every aspect of human existence. As for the individual, so for the nation: we reap what we sow. Israel had to learn the hard way that breaking the commands of God eventually leads to national disaster.

The prophets of Israel have much to say about the use and abuse of material wealth. Isaiah warns that those who have gained their riches by oppressing the poor and the widow will find that their wealth will not protect them from the wrath of God's judgment (Isa. 10:1-3). Jeremiah tells of the time when treasures gained through injustice will be handed over to the enemies of Israel (Jer. 5:27; 15:13). The wise man should not glory in his wisdom, nor the mighty man in his might, nor the rich man in his riches; but the truly wise man should glory in the knowledge of God's revealed character and requirements for a righteous way of life (9:23,24). Ezekiel warns that wealth derived from injustice, pride, and violence will not escape the judgment of a holy God (Ezek. 7:11). Hosea reminds

Israel that material abundance cannot compensate for the great weight of moral guilt in the sight of God (Hos. 12:8). Amos condemns those who trample upon the poor for the sake of economic gain and calls for "justice [to] roll down like waters, and righteousness like an everflowing stream" (Amos 5:11, 24). Like his predecessors, Micah cries out against riches gained by violence (Mic. 6:12).

The prophets of Israel neither condemn wealth itself nor exalt poverty as a moral ideal. They do, however, clearly attest that great wealth, like great power or learning, can be abused. They would not agree with the cynical observation that "behind every great fortune lies a great crime." Contrary to the view that great wealth is gained only through dishonesty and injustice, they consistently teach that wealth is to be gained only in a righteous manner and is to be used in a compassionate way that alleviates the suffering of the less fortunate. "Is not this the fast that I choose . . . to share your bread with the hungry, and bring the homeless poor into your house?" (Isa. 58:6).

Calvin Coolidge was certainly not a prophet, but the prophets would have concurred with the American President when he remarked, "Prosperity is only an instrument to be used, not a deity to be worshipped." The temptation for God's people to serve Mammon rather than God is all too real.

The books of Psalms and Proverbs are rich with insights about the nature of temporal prosperity. The psalmists are realistic enough to recognize that at times great wealth may result from unrighteous practices rather than the direct blessing of God. The author of Psalm 10 observes that "the man greedy for gain renounces the Lord . . . his ways prosper at all times." The writer recognizes that in this life the wicked often do not receive the swift and immediate divine judgment their deeds deserve. The Mafia's economic assets are certainly no sign of divine approval. While disparities and injustices are plentiful in a sinful world, the psalmists know that those who trust wealth rather than God have placed their faith in a transient and fleeting quantity. Wealth cannot ransom sinners from death, but the faithful have the confidence that God will receive them into his eternal fellowship: "Why should I fear in times of trouble, when the iniquity of my persecutors surrounds me," asks the author of Psalm 49, "men who trust in their wealth and boast of the abundance of their riches?" The psalmist takes heart in the fact that "no man can ransom himself, or give to God the price of his life. . . . But God will ransom my soul from the power of Sheol, for he will receive me." Death, which from one perspective is the great equalizer, in the perspective of eternity is the ultimate crisis, which vindicates the righteous against the wicked.

It would be wrong, however, to suppose the psalms teach that the unrighteous prosper invariably or even most of the time. The author of Psalm 112 speaks of the temporal blessings enjoyed by a righteous man who fears the Lord, delights in his commandments, conducts his affairs with justice, and is generous to the poor: "Wealth and riches are in his house; and his righteousness endures forever. . . . It is well with the man who deals generously and lends" (vv. 3,5). Likewise, Psalm 128 speaks of God's blessing on those who fear the Lord and walk in his ways: "You shall eat the fruit of the labor of your hands; you shall be happy, and it shall be well with you" (v. 2).

Some of the most extensive teaching in Scripture concerning wealth and prosperity is found in the book of Proverbs. Ultimately, wealth and the ability to gain and enjoy it are gifts of God (10:22). On the human side, wealth is the result of industrious labor: "The sluggard craves, and has nothing, but the soul of the diligent is richly supplied" (13:4). "In all toil there is profit, but mere talk leads only to poverty" (14:23). "A slack hand causes poverty, but the hand of the diligent makes rich" (10:4). Without question the book of Proverbs endorses the "work ethic" and a life characterized by diligence, energetic effort, and self-discipline. The experience of mankind has shown that individuals and cultures characterized by such virtues have in fact tended to prosper. In recent years non-Christian societies such as Japan, Singapore, and Hong Kong have outwardly conformed to the principles of Proverbs more consistently than have nations like our own, which can claim a biblical heritage. The need is urgent for believers, who are called to be the salt of the earth and the light of the world, to show diligence and energy in their own places of employment.

Professor Theodore Schultz of the University of Chicago was awarded the Nobel Prize in economics for his studies in "human capital formation." Sent to Germany after the Second World War to study the process of reconstruction, Schultz found that while the nation's industrial plants and machinery were in shambles, the German people still possessed the knowledge and will to become a major world economic power again. He concluded that Germany's disciplined and energetic work force was a crucial element in the nation's economic recovery.[4] Professor Schultz found that the key difference between declining economies and advancing economies was not so much in natural resources as in human resources. This crucial link between human character, productivity, and prosperity confirms the wisdom of Proverbs.

While the proverbs teach a very strong appreciation of wealth, they also place significant moral restraints on the means of its acquisition. Wealth is not to be gained through deceit (21:6), by the use of false weights (20:10), by shifting landmarkers (22:28), or through oppression (23:10-11). Wealth unjustly gained will prove to be a "fleeting vapor and a snare of death" (21:6).

While wealth can be a blessing, it should not be overvalued. It is not to become the final object of the believer's trust (11:28). The righteous are reminded to "honor the Lord with your substance, and with the first fruits of all your produce" (3:9). The righteous will be generous in giving to the needs of others (3:27,28), realizing that being kind to the poor is a way of lending to the Lord (19:17). If a choice must be made between riches and a good reputation, then the latter is clearly of greater value: "A good name is to be chosen rather than great riches, and favor is better than silver or gold" (22:1). Wealth has its benefits, but Proverbs admonishes the reader to remember that wisdom "is more precious than jewels, and nothing you desire can compare with her" (3:15)—the divine wisdom, revealed in Jesus Christ, in whom are hidden all God's treasures of wisdom and knowledge (Col. 2:3).

Seeking First the Kingdom: Wealth in the New Testament

As one would expect, there is basic agreement between the Old and New Testament perspectives on wealth. Jesus himself said that he came not to abolish the law and the prophets, but to fulfil them (Matt. 5:17). At the same time, his emphasis on the kingdom of God underscores that all temporal concerns fade into the background when compared to the eternal issues of life, death, judgment, and salvation. The message of the kingdom requires men and women to refocus their personal priorities in the light of eternity: "Seek first the kingdom of God and his righteousness, and all these other things shall be yours as well" (Matt. 6:33). The kingdom of God is of such transcendent value that one should be willing to sell all in order to possess it (Matt. 13:44-46; cf. 19:16-30, the rich young ruler).

Jesus warns his disciples about the danger of letting riches compete with the demands of the kingdom for their deepest loyalty. Rather than concentrating on laying up treasures on earth, the disciples are to lay up treasures in heaven through acts of faith and obedience, for one's "treasure" sets the direction of one's life (Matt. 6:19-21). As the New Testament scholar David Hill has observed, "Each individual sets his heart on what he counts important, and this allegiance determines the direction and content of his life."[5] While the words of Jesus are not intended to rule out bank accounts, pension plans, and responsible planning for the future (in that a believer is responsible for taking care of his own family—I Tim. 5:8), Matthew 6 makes it clear that one's life is not to be oriented toward the love of money.

Jesus warns that a delight in riches and a worldly spirit can block spiritual growth and fruitfulness (Mark 4:19). No one can serve two masters; the believer cannot serve both God and money (Matt. 6:24). As Colin Brown explains, "Mammon . . . inevitably becomes the master if a man tries to make himself its master by acquiring it for its own sake."[6] Again, Jesus is not teaching that money itself or the lawful earning of money in business enterprise is evil, but rather that God and not wealth must always come first in the believer's heart and life. It would be the height of folly to spend one's life heaping up possessions, for true life does not consist in the abundance of possessions (Luke 12:15).

The parables of Jesus are rich with insights concerning the responsibilities of Christian stewardship. In the parable of the unrighteous steward (Luke 16:1-13) the point is made that believers should use their money in ways that promote acceptance with God and the neighbor: "Make friends for yourselves by means of the unrighteous mammon," by being shrewd and generous rather than miserly in its use. As Johannes Eichler and Colin Brown have put it, the point is that "what is worth possessing is not material things which perish but personal acceptance by God and by those who have benefited from one's use of material things."[7]

The parable of the talents (Matt. 25:14-30) shows clearly that God's people are to be wise and energetic in using the resources their Master has entrusted to them. The slothful servant is rebuked for burying his talent in the ground; at the very least, he should have invested the money with the bankers so that his master would have received interest (v. 27). The entire parable presupposes the legitimacy of lawful business endeavors. Those who have been diligent and faithful will be rewarded by the master and given even more challenging places of service (v. 23).

Christ intends economic activity to be a school of character for the Christian. The one who is faithful in little things will also prove faithful in the greater things; economic responsibility trains us for responsibility in the things of eternity (Luke 16:10, 11). As Calvin Coolidge commented in another context, "Industry, thrift, and self-control are not sought because they create wealth, but because they create character."[8]

While Jesus spoke with stark realism about the risks of great wealth, he never taught that poverty itself is a sign of spiritual merit. Although many of the poor will be more blessed than the rich (cf. Luke 6:17-26), the cause of their blessedness is their faith in the gospel, not their poverty. The poor widow who gave all that she had is praised not for her poverty, but for the sincerity and depth of her devotion to God (Mark 12:41-44). Whatever one's circumstances, the "one thing necessary" is seeking first the kingdom of God, putting God first in every area of life.

The attitudes toward wealth in the early church and the teaching of the apostles consistently reflect those of Jesus. Property sharing in the Jerusalem church (Acts 4:32-35) provided a vivid illustration of the believers' love for one another. While the practice of communal property was evidently a temporary one and not made obligatory by the apostles for other churches (cf. Acts 15:22-29), the apostles consistently taught that Christians should share generously to meet urgent needs within the fellowship. Paul, for example, urged the Corinthians to give generously and voluntarily to the collection for the poor in the Jerusalem church. "As a matter of equity, your abundance should supply their want" (II Cor. 8:14). James reminds his readers that a "faith" that does not assist a brother or sister in urgent need is a dead faith (James 2:14-17). The apostle John asks, "If anyone has the world's goods and sees his brother in need, yet closes his heart against him, how does the love of God abide in him?" (I John 3:17). Members of the fellowship are to express love not in word only, but "in deed and in truth."

The transforming power of the gospel can overcome social divisions between rich and poor within the church. In the fellowship of Jesus Christ, both Jew and Greek, slave and free, enjoy a fundamental spiritual equality by the grace of God (Gal. 3:28). This truth was at times imperfectly realized in the apostolic church, as is the case today. James needed to remind his readers that showing partiality in the church toward the wealthy was contrary to the new standards of the kingdom (James 2:1-7).

The kingdom of God broke into history with a powerful effect on the early church's perception of the place of wealth and possessions in the believer's life. The light of the eternal realities of the gospel makes it obvious that temporal wealth has only a relative importance. Paul advised the Corinthians to hold their possessions lightly, "for the form of this world is passing away" (I Cor. 7:31). Because his relationship with the living Christ produced unmatched personal fulfillment, Paul could be content in all circumstances, whether in wealth or in poverty (Phil. 4:11, 12). In Christ he knew a contentment not dependent on the changing fortunes of outward circumstance. These same insights are found in Paul's words to Timothy, when he reminds his young assistant that "there is great gain in godliness with contentment. . . . if we have food and clothing, with these we shall be content" (I Tim. 6:6,8). Such counsel is not easy to keep in focus in a consumer society, but the apostle's words represent a continuing challenge to the church to keep the eternal and the temporal dimensions of the Christian life in proper perspective.

Some time ago we took a family trip to Portsmouth, New Hampshire, and as we were leaving the city, we happened to pass a large scrap metal collection center not far from the waterfront. We stopped for a while to watch a stream of dump trucks bring piles of metal to the site where a large crane with an electromagnet scoop was building a heap several stories high. Among the rusty heap we could see what appeared to be the remains of refrigerators, cars, appliances, and a myriad of other once-glistening products of our industrial economy. As we sat there I recalled a sermon by Dr. Francis Schaeffer entitled, "Ash Heap Lives," in which he underscored from Scripture the futility of building one's life around material things, which are ultimately destined for the junk yard. As the apostle Paul put it, "we brought nothing into the world, and we cannot take anything out of the world" (I Tim. 6:7). An occasional trip to a junk yard can help a person keep the temporal and eternal things of life in proper balance.

It would be a mistake, however, to conclude that the apostles scorned the good things of this life. Paul did not *deliberately* seek to be abased, and he knew how to enjoy times of abundance, when God provided them (Phil. 4:12). In the same letter to Timothy where he reminds us that "you can't take it with you," he also teaches that "everything created by God is good, and nothing is to be rejected if it is received with thanksgiving; for then it is consecrated by the word of God and prayer" (I Tim. 4:4,5). The New Testament neither endorses a world-scorning asceticism, for such an attitude denies the goodness of God's creation, nor scorns wealth itself. Rather than condemning the "rich in this world" (I Tim. 6:17) for being wealthy, Paul instructs them to be "rich in good deeds," generously giving to those in less fortunate circumstances. Likewise James does not condemn the wealthy because they have more money than others in the church, but because, in that case, their gains were obtained through injustice and fraud (James 5:1-6). As the New Testament scholar Gordon Fee has put it, the New Testament "does not require poverty, but it does require righteousness, which . . . means to use our wealth not to manipulate others, but to alleviate the hurt and pain of the oppressed."

Wealth and the Christian Life: Some Concluding Questions

Is there a dramatic shift in views on wealth from the Old Testament to the New? Is it true, as one writer is reported to have said, that "in the Old Testament God's blessing is seen in material abundance, while in the New God's blessings are seen in adversity"? Are the Old Testament promises of obedience and blessing still valid today?

It seems undeniable that in the balance between temporal and eternal concerns, the New Testament clearly concentrates on the eternal. That is to be expected, since the ministry of Jesus Christ was a fundamental turning point in history as the plan of God came to a climax: "The time is *fulfilled,* and the kingdom of God is *at hand*" (Mark 1:15). In light of the radical demands of the gospel, temporal concerns became secondary as eternity hung in the balance.

At the same time, it is important to see the fundamental continuity between the testaments. Both parts of the biblical canon insist on personal priorities that put God first. Just as Jesus commands his disciples to seek first the kingdom of God and his righteousness (Matt. 6:33), the psalmist declares that the law of God is more precious than thousands of gold and silver pieces (Ps. 119:72). The Old Testament both teaches a clear connection between national righteousness and material blessing (Deut. 28) and shows that a righteous individual, such as Jeremiah, who serves God in the midst of an unrighteous culture will suffer temporal adversity. The general principle of Deuteronomy 28 still holds good in national life, as subsequent history tends to show. Nations that have been significantly influenced by biblical teaching, such as the lands of the Protestant Reformation, have tended to be more prosperous than nations such as India, where the gospel has not yet made a deep impact. While it is true that Israel was a theocracy and modern nations are not, nevertheless Israel was intended to be a "light to the nations," a model to all nations of the benefits of serving the true and living God.

Both testaments commend diligence and the value of hard work. The Old Testament teaches that a slack hand causes poverty (Prov. 10:4), and the New Testament commands the believer to work in quietness and earn his own living (II Thess. 3:12). Because of historical and societal factors beyond his control, a diligent believer in Russia may be prevented from enjoying the material rewards he might otherwise have enjoyed in America, but the difference is due to circumstances, not to some dramatic shift in biblical principles. Obedience, diligence, and self-discipline remain important Christian virtues. "Godliness is of value in every way, as it holds promise *for the present life* and also for the life to come" (I Tim. 4:8).

Does the Bible condemn the mere possession of surplus wealth? Are American Christians automatically guilty in God's sight because their standard of living is higher than millions of others in a world where poverty is common?

There is certainly no question that Scripture teaches a moral obligation to give generously to the needs of the poor. Job was a righteous man who delivered the poor when they cried for help (Job 29:12). We are not to withhold help from our neighbor when it is possible for us to assist (Prov. 3:27,28). Those who are kind to the poor give honor to God their Creator (Prov. 14:31). The virtuous woman reaches out her hands to the needy (Prov. 31:20). The true worship of God involves caring for the hungry and the homeless poor (Isa. 58:6,7). As we have opportunity, we are to do good to all men, especially those who are of the household of faith (Gal. 6:10).

At the same time, as we have already noted, individuals such as Abraham, Isaac, Jacob, Solomon, and Job were blessed by God with surplus wealth. From Scripture as a whole it seems clear that the real issue is not the mere quantity of wealth one possesses, but one's attitude toward it and use of it. Job was a wealthy man who gave generously to the poor, while the rich man described in Luke 16 is condemned for selfishly ignoring the needs of poor Lazarus at his doorstep. When the apostle Paul instructs the wealthy to be generous in their giving, he does not condemn them for merely possessing surplus wealth (I Tim. 6:18). Any Christian may, of course, voluntarily choose to live at a subsistence level in order to give more money to the poor and the work of spreading the gospel; and some people have a special calling from God to do so. But to make this a requirement that binds the conscience of all Christians is a form of legalism, which is contrary to the teaching of Scripture as a whole.

It is important to distinguish accumulation motivated by greed and covetousness from the legitimate capital accumulation associated with saving for the needs of one's family or the normal operations of a business enterprise. Greed and covetousness are clearly sinful (Exod. 20:17; Luke 12:15; Col. 3:5). But saving for legitimate future needs is clearly different from covetousness and is commended by Scripture. We are admonished to learn wisdom from the ant, who, in summer, stores food for his winter needs (Prov. 6:6-8). A good man leaves an inheritance to his children's children (Prov. 13:22). The one who does not provide for the needs of his own family has denied the faith, and is worse than an unbeliever (I Tim. 5:8).

Legitimate capital formation in business should not be confused with greed. In order to remain competitive, businesses must accumulate capital to invest in new plants and equipment. Without such saving and investment a firm's ability to provide goods and services to the public and employment to the workers will be eroded over time. In the parable of the talents (Matt. 25:14-30) the servants are expected not to give all their resources to the poor, but to manage and invest their resources for the master's profit. While individual acts of benevolence are needed to provide immediate relief to individuals in need, business enterprises can provide more lasting solutions to the problem of poverty. A successful business provides not only a source of income and employment, but also a context in which the individual can learn the character traits of responsibility and self-discipline, which are essential for economic well-being.

Finally, what are we to make of the so-called "gospel of prosperity"? What of the radio preachers whose message is, in effect, "serve God and get rich"? Among their favorite verses are III John 2, "Beloved, I wish above all things that thou mayest prosper," and

John 10:10, which states that Christ came that we might have life, and have it abundantly. Both verses are taken out of their proper context. The words of III John 2 were a standardized form of greeting in the letters of antiquity, somewhat similar to our expression, "Have a nice day," and can hardly be generalized to promise financial prosperity to all Christians in all ages and circumstances. With respect to the abundant life of John 10:10, it is clear from the Gospel of John as a whole that the focus is not on material circumstances, but on the eternal life and forgiveness of sins that comes through faith in Jesus Christ (3:16; 5:24; 6:40; 11:25; 14:6).

That is not to deny the scriptural connections between obedience, diligence, and temporal blessing. But different circumstances can lead to different outward results for two believers who are equally faithful. Both Abraham and Jeremiah were righteous men, but because God called them to live in different times and circumstances, one was notably wealthy, and the other was not. A Christian living in Russia or Poland may be just as faithful and diligent as a Christian living in America or Singapore, and yet, because of the social conditions in which he lives, not be allowed to enjoy the full benefits of his labor. One faithful Christian may be blessed with temporal prosperity, and another may be called to serve God through persecution and even martyrdom.

The focus in Scripture is on serving God and enjoying the riches of salvation. Material wealth is not to be despised and may be entrusted to us for a time, but it must never be allowed to become the primary concern of life. The sentiments expressed by Theodore Roosevelt in a Fourth of July message in 1886 are very much in keeping with the spirit of Scripture: "I do not undervalue for a moment our material prosperity. . . . But we must keep steadily in mind that no people were ever benefitted by riches if their prosperity corrupted their virtue."[9]

The highest goal in the Christian life is to seek first the kingdom of God in all things, to seek spiritual growth and moral conformity to the image of Jesus Christ (Rom. 8:29). The Christian's true commonwealth is in heaven (Phil. 3:20), where there abides a precious inheritance that can never fade away (I Pet. 1:4).

3

Poverty: Justice, Compassion, and Personal Responsibility

"In one world, as in one state, when I am rich because you are poor, and I am poor because you are rich, the transfer of wealth from the rich to the poor is a matter of rights; it is not an appropriate matter for charity."[1] Such are the angry claims of Julius Nyerere, president of the African nation of Tanzania. His sentiments are echoed by the Third-World revolutionary Frantz Fanon: "The question which is looming on the horizon is the need for a redistribution of wealth. Humanity must reply to this question, or be shaken to pieces by it."[2]

Are the charges of Nyerere and Fanon supported by the facts and by the teachings of the Bible? Do we as members of the more affluent nations have a moral obligation to give "reparations" to the poor of the Third- and Fourth-World nations? Does our wealth cause their poverty? Is it true, as some prominent Christian leaders are saying, that "God is on the side of the poor"? According to the Bible, what are the basic causes of poverty?

The frequency of such claims and counterclaims in Christian circles today makes it all the more necessary to examine carefully the teachings of Scripture on the subject of poverty. Without such a grounding in the teaching of Scripture, the Christian is open to the twin dangers of either neglecting true responsibilities to exercise compassion or being manipulated by a false feeling of guilt.

The World Outlook

Before examining the biblical data, we need to recall some basic facts about past and present poverty for the sake of gaining perspective. As twentieth-century Americans, it is easy to forget that poverty has been the normal lot of the vast majority of mankind for most of recorded history. The economic writer Henry Hazlitt has observed, "The history of poverty is almost the history of mankind."[3]

Poverty was the order of the day in the ancient world. Greek dwellings had no heat in winter, no adequate sanitary arrangements, and no washing facilities. The average Roman house was little better. Recurring famines took thousands of lives. In a famine in Rome in 436 B.C., thousands of starving people threw themselves into the Tiber River, so great was their desperation.[4]

General and widespread poverty was also characteristic of the Middle Ages. "Alternations between feastings and starvation, famines, crime, violence, scurvy, leprosy, typhoid, wars, pestilence and plague were part of medieval life to an extent we can hardly imagine today," wrote historian E. Parmalee Prentice. The homes of typical medieval laborers were hovels. The walls were made of boards cemented with mud and leaves; there was no sewage or water supply. The entire family was crowded into a single room or perhaps two, together with the family's animals.[5]

The *Encyclopaedia Britannica* listed some 31 major famines from ancient times down through 1960. Famines are still common in the less developed countries. In modern socialist nations food shortages are a recurring problem, as this recent headline attested: "Rationing of Sugar and Meat in Poland."

The fact of poverty as the "normal" condition of the human race began to change with the rise of the Industrial Revolution in the mid-eighteenth century. Through the benefits of modern science and technology, poverty in Western industrial nations has been changed from the *normal* condition of the *majority* to the *abnormal* condition of a shrinking *minority*. It is easy to forget what a dramatic change this transformation has meant for the average person. The less developed nations are responding to a "revolution of rising expectations" created by the advances of the Industrial Revolution.

Here in the United States substantial progress has been made in efforts to reduce poverty to a residual level. Warren Brookes, economic writer for the *Boston Herald American*, has called attention to the fact that "in spite of spiraling inflation, and energy costs, socioeconomic data now shows that less than 7 percent of all Americans live below the U.S. poverty line, and even this 7 percent live better than 85 percent of the rest of the world's population." While it may be true that the United States, with only 6 percent of the world's population, uses over a third of the world's energy, Brookes points out that the critics usually fail to mention that the United States produces 40 percent of the world's food and supports nearly 80 percent of the world's private charities.[6]

Dr. Michael J. Boskin, a professor of economics at Stanford University, has recently called attention to features of the government's "poverty index" that tend to exaggerate the size of the problem. While the index is adjusted for inflation, family size, and location, it excludes the actual cash value of transfer payments such as food stamps, subsidized housing, and medical care. "Even conservative estimates of the cash-equivalent value of these programs result in a startling discovery," writes Professor Boskin; "only about 3 percent of Americans live below the poverty line."[7] If Boskin's analysis is correct, then the "war on poverty" in America is a war that has practically been won.

In the world as a whole, it is undeniable that there are multitudes of poor and hungry people. But there are signs of hope, and well-meaning reformers at times inadvertently exaggerate the magnitude of the problem.

In a recent issue of *Commentary*, Nick Eberstadt argued that the figure of 30 million children dying of starvation each year quoted by World Bank president Robert McNamara was four times too high. The World Bank figures failed to take into account local variations in

caloric needs. With the World Bank's methodology, caloric depriva-
tion would be ascribed to 48 percent of the population in Taiwan and
to 40 percent in Hong Kong, but life expectancy in both places is over
72—about the same as in Finland or Austria.[8]

The world hunger situation has shown signs of improvement. In
the past 30 years, life expectancy in the less-developed countries,
excluding China, has risen by more than a third, and China's may be
up by 50 percent. Since 1950, worldwide per-capita food production has risen by about 40 percent, in spite of dramatic population
growth. Between 1950 and 1980, the world's arable land area grew
by more than 20 percent, and even more rapidly in the poor countries as a whole.[9] These figures do not minimize the tragic propor-
tions of the hunger and poverty that still exist, but they do caution
against careless exaggerations that in the long run only retard responsible measures necessary to alleviate the problems.

The experience of the modern Asian states of Taiwan, Singapore,
Hong Kong, and South Korea demonstrates that determined and
energetic societies can overcome conditions of poverty. These once-
poor societies have been notably transformed in the last 20 years
through initiative and hard work. Singapore, a city-state hardly
larger than Memphis, Tennessee, and without natural resources,
has won 25 percent of the global backlog of orders for oil rigs, second
only to the United States. South Korea is already the world's largest
producer of black and white television sets. These Asian states are
rapidly moving from traditional reliance on the manufacture of
cheap garments and toys into the high technology areas, offering
stiff competition to Japan.[10] Their experience shows that poverty
can be overcome not through exploiting others, but through initiative, enterprise, efficiency, and hard work.

Biblical Insights

The teachings of Scripture give a balanced perspective on the
subject of poverty. On the one hand, poverty in general is
considered an undesirable and unfortunate circumstance. To wish
someone to become poor can be a form of cursing (II Sam. 3:29—

David's curse on Joab for the murder of Abner; Ps. 109:9-10—David's prayer of imprecation against his persecutors). On the other hand, Scripture makes clear that character is more important than circumstances. A life of poverty with integrity is to be preferred to ill-gotten wealth (Prov. 28:6). The wisdom literature of the Bible commends a moderate life situation characterized by neither wealth nor poverty: "Give me neither poverty nor riches; feed me with the food that is needful for me, lest I be full, and deny thee, and say, 'Who is the Lord?' or lest I be poor, and steal, and profane the name of my God" (Prov. 30:9). This teaching is consistent with the Pauline admonition to be content with the necessities of life (I Tim. 6:6-8), since the Christian's true fulfillment is found not in outward possessions, but in a personal relationship with the risen Lord.

God's concern for the needs of the poor is evident throughout the Bible. God pities and comforts the poor (Ps. 34:6; Isa. 49:13), and actively cares for them (Job 5:15; Ps. 107:41). The God of Israel actively seeks social justice for the poor and the oppressed. The Lord "executes justice for the fatherless and the widow, and loves the sojourner, giving him food and clothing" (Deut. 10:18). Israel is commanded to love the sojourner, and to remember its own experience of poverty and sojourning in Egypt. The God of Israel is a "stronghold to the poor, a stronghold to the needy in his distress" (Isa. 25:4).

The legal sections of the Old Testament contained special provisions for the needs of the poor. The poor were to be allowed to glean in the fields and the vineyards (Lev. 19:9, 10; 23:22; Deut. 24:19). The right of gleaning provided a meager source of food for the needy, but the personal effort involved in the process—unlike some modern welfare systems—discouraged idleness and sloth.

The tithe of the third year was to be set aside for the poor and needy. "At the end of every three years you shall bring forth all the tithe of your produce in the same year, and lay it up within your towns; and the Levite, because he has no portion or inheritance with you, and the sojourner, the fatherless, and the widow, who are within your towns, shall come and eat and be filled; that the Lord your God may bless you in all the work of your hands that you do"

(Deut. 14:28,29). God's people were promised a blessing for faithfully tithing in order to alleviate the distress of the poor.

The poor of Israel were also allowed to present less expensive offerings at the temple (Lev. 12:8; 14:21; 27:8). Evidently Joseph and Mary were in this category when they brought the baby Jesus to be presented in the temple (Luke 2:22-24).

Hebrew judges were to give the poor full protection. "You shall not pervert justice; you shall not show partiality" (Deut. 16:14); "give justice to the weak and the fatherless" (Ps. 82:3).

In some Christian circles it is said that "God is on the side of the poor." This type of language, while echoing biblical themes, can be misleading. While, as we have already seen, God is *concerned* for the *needs* of the poor, he is by no means partial to the poor in matters of criminal justice. Old Testament law expressly teaches the very opposite: "Nor shall you be partial to a poor man in his suit" (Exod. 23:3). "You shall do no injustice in judgment; you shall not be partial to the poor or defer to the great, but in righteousness you shall judge your neighbor" (Lev. 19:15). Since God is no respecter of persons, he judges guilt and innocence apart from outward circumstances, whether wealth or poverty. Some evangelical "liberation theologians," in their apparent bias toward the cause of the poor, overlook the teachings of Exodus 23:3 and Leviticus 19:15.

In the New Testament, Jesus showed concern for the poor (Matt. 19:21; John 13:29), and commended the giving of alms (Mark 12:42-44). One of the blessings of the new age was that the poor would have the gospel preached to them (Matt. 11:5; Luke 14:21). At the same time, Jesus made it clear that his primary mission was not to alleviate hunger and physical suffering—though he did much of that—but to die for the sins of the lost (John 6:27; Mark 10:45).

The early church cared for its own poor (Acts 2:45; 4:34; 11:29). Widows who had no other means of support were to be cared for by the church (I Tim. 5:16). Families were to take care of their own, and children were to help their elderly parents (I Tim. 5:4-8). If the Christian church were to consistently apply these provisions today, much of the taxation for social welfare programs would be unnecessary.

32   *Your Wealth in God's World*

The apostle Paul took with utmost seriousness his task of administering a collection from the Gentile churches for the needy saints in Jerusalem (II Cor. 8; Gal. 2:10). Such giving was a tangible sign of the spiritual unity of the new fellowship in Christ that included both Jew and Gentile.

In both testaments kindness to the poor is honoring to God (Prov. 14:31; cf. Luke 14:13-14). When the believer comprehends the magnitude of God's gift to him in Christ, then a life characterized by giving to the needs of others is the natural result (II Cor. 8:9; 9:8).

The Causes of Poverty

One popular theory about the cause of poverty might be called the "robber baron" theory. According to this theory, if I am rich and you are poor, it must be that you have been the victim of my exploitation and oppression. That view was popularized by Karl Marx, who believed that the relationship between capital and labor was inherently that of oppressor and oppressed.

Surely both Scripture and experience show that the poor can be exploited by the rich. The prophet Amos condemned those in his own day who sold "the needy for a pair of shoes . . . and trampled the head of the poor into the dust of the earth" (2:6, 7). The prophet Isaiah declared, "The Lord enters into judgment with the elders and princes of the people: 'It is you who have devoured the vineyard, the spoil of the poor is in your houses. What do you mean by crushing my people, by grinding the faces of the poor?' " (3:14, 15). In the New Testament, James condemns wealthy landowners who have defrauded their workers: "Behold, the wages of the laborers who mowed your fields, which you have kept back by fraud, cry out; and the cries of the harvesters have reached the ears of the Lord of hosts" (5:4). The fact of oppression in human experience cannot be denied, and it is common enough to make the robber baron theory plausible. We have heard such sentiments voiced by Julius Nyerere of Tanzania in the words quoted at the beginning of this chapter.

It would be a fatal error, however, to believe that *all* poverty is the result of oppression. Neither Scripture nor experience supports such a theory. The robber baron theory misunderstands the nature of both wealth and a free exchange in the market economy, and it slanders the character of those who have become wealthy through personal initiative, insight, and hard work.

Most wealth today is derived neither from exploitation nor from digging material resources out of the ground, but from discovering new ways of producing goods, organizing work, or processing information. As Max Singer and Paul Bracken of the Hudson Institute have observed, "Much modern wealth isn't based on things at all, but on ideas, techniques, information, and other intangibles, such as new ways of motivating people or organizing work." They note that Japan's economic success "is the most dramatic evidence that wealth does not have to be based on natural resources."[11]

The invention of the computer chip has spawned a whole new industry and created thousands of new jobs. The computer chip represents a new source of wealth derived not from exploitation, but from human inventiveness that transformed ordinary sand into an instrument for processing information faster and more efficiently and in a tinier space.

The latest development along these lines is the "seeing eye" or "imager" chip. In a growing number of lumber mills logs are sized up by imager-chip cameras linked to computers that control the cutting saws. The result is five to ten percent more lumber per log. Again, the gain is the product not of exploitation, but of human creativity.

Notice also that a free enterprise economy is based on *free exchange*. The Beatles freely chose to write music and produce records, and millions of young people freely chose to exchange their money for those records. One may or may not like the music of the Beatles, but it must be granted that they became millionaires many times over not through theft and fraud, but by freely producing a product that millions freely chose to purchase. A genuinely free exchange is not a "zero-sum" or "I win, you lose" situation, but a relationship in which both parties benefit. Unless both parties value what they receive more than what they give up, the exchange will not take place. The teenager valued the record more than the money required to purchase it; and the producer, the money more than the record. In a free exchange, disturbed by neither force nor fraud, both parties benefit and increase their sense of personal satisfaction. The robber baron or "rip-off" theory of poverty and wealth fails to understand the dynamics of a free exchange economy.

Another popular but mistaken idea today is that the wealth of Western nations is the cause of the poverty in Third-World nations. This contention is simply not supported by the facts. Some of the most affluent nations, such as Switzerland and Sweden, never had any colonies at all. Others, such as Germany and Japan, became wealthy only after losing their colonies. Some of the most economically underdeveloped nations—Afghanistan, Tibet, Nepal, Liberia—never were colonies of the West.[12] And in general, the most economically advanced Third-World nations today are precisely those having had the most extensive contact with the West.

As Professor P. T. Bauer of the London School of Economics has pointed out, "Before colonial rule there was not a single cocoa tree in the Gold Coast [Ghana]; when colonial rule ended, cocoa exports, entirely from African-owned and operated farms, totaled hundreds of thousands of tons annually." In the 1890s, Malaya was a sparsely populated land of fishing villages and hamlets. "By the 1930's," notes Bauer, "it had become a country with populous cities, thriving commerce, and an excellent system of roads, primarily thanks to the rubber industry brought there and developed by the British."[13]

The fact of the matter is that the colonial system benefitted the colonies as well as the ruling countries. Colonization brought schools, roads, banking, and business know-how without which much of the former colonies' present economic development would have been impossible. Resentful robber-baron theories applied to the West by Third-World leaders influenced by Marxist ideology distort the historical record and short-circuit the personal initiative needed for upward economic mobility in their societies.

While Scripture clearly recognizes that poverty may be caused or aggravated by external circumstances such as oppression and injustice, it teaches just as clearly that individual character is a crucial factor influencing one's state of poverty or affluence. Poverty can be caused by sloth and laziness. "A little sleep, a little slumber, a little folding of the hands to rest, and poverty will come upon you like a vagabond, and want like an armed man" (Prov. 6:10, 11). "Slothfulness casts into a deep sleep, and an idle person will suffer hunger" (Prov. 19:15). The sluggard neglects his own fields and vineyards, and suffers impoverishment as a result (Prov. 24:30-34).

The Scriptures call all people to assume personal responsibility for their own lives and circumstances, rather than depend on government for their basic needs. Instead of blaming impersonal environmental and structural conditions for one's poverty, individuals are urged to take personal initiative and actively exert the effort necessary to better their circumstances.

In 1966, Professor James S. Coleman stunned the educational world with his massive study, *Equality of Educational Opportunity*, perhaps the second most expensive social research project in U.S. history. The conclusion of Coleman's study was that public schools made no measurable impact either in eliminating or even in modifying disparity of achievement among students. That was a stunning blow to the liberal assumptions undergirding U.S. social and educational policy during the 1960s, namely, that spending more money on the public schools would reduce poverty. That assumption saw the primary roots of poverty in the child's social environment. Coleman's findings pointed instead to *family values* as the prime factor in educational achievement. It turned out that the character formation provided by a sound family structure, rather than "federal money thrown at a social problem" was the key to motivation and achievement in the public schools—a result that biblically oriented Christians could have suspected all along.

The Bible points to other character traits that can cause impoverishment. Folly and stubbornness can bring one to such a state: "Poverty and disgrace come to him who ignores instruction" (Prov. 13:18). "He who tills his land will have plenty to eat, but he who follows worthless pursuits will have plenty of poverty" (Prov. 28:19). A hedonistic lifestyle can bring one to poverty: "He who loves pleasure will be a poor man; he who loves wine and oil will not be rich" (Prov. 21:17).

In 1970, Professor Edward Banfield of Harvard earned the wrath of much of the academic profession with his book, *The Unheavenly City.* Banfield argued, contrary to the conventional wisdom, that the primary cause of poverty in the ghetto is not external but internal, and in particular, the self-chosen lifestyle of the majority of ghetto inhabitants. The problem according to Banfield is "present orientation," a set of values oriented toward "action" and immediate gratification, rather than planning, saving, and extended effort. Such a value orientation cannot be changed merely by bigger schools or better job training, but only through a more fundamental moral and spiritual reorientation—a "conversion." Banfield's insights reflect the truth of Proverbs 21:17 and underscore the fact that poverty is basically rooted in a state of mind rather than in external circumstances.

James A. Michener once said, "I still believe hard work is the salvation for many of us and one of the principal agencies whereby our society achieves its goals."[14] While an evangelical would certainly want to qualify Michener's use of the term "salvation," we could still agree that personal effort and character as keys to achievement are firmly grounded in the teachings of Scripture.

The biblical connection between character and economic circumstances applies to nations as well as to individuals. In an earlier chapter we saw how Deuteronomy 28 promised temporal blessing as a result of national righteousness, and temporal impoverishment as a result of disobedience. This was amply confirmed in the life of Israel, as the books of Haggai and Joel demonstrate.

It is intriguing to study modern history and notice how nations such as the United States, Canada, England, Germany, the Scandinavian countries, and Switzerland, which were significantly affected by the Protestant Reformation, have enjoyed greater economic prosperity than nations such as Spain, Portugal, and Italy, where Catholicism has been the dominant religion. Many factors were at work, of course, but nevertheless the sense of personal responsibility encouraged by the Reformation gospel was a powerful stimulus to economic improvement.

One of the ironies of the modern world is that the "Protestant work ethic" seems best exemplified in non-Christian states such as Japan, Singapore, South Korea, Taiwan, and Hong Kong. Insofar as these new industrial giants of Asia have applied virtues commended by the Bible, they have enjoyed remarkable economic prosperity. Their experience does not confirm a doctrine of "salvation by works," but it does bear out that God attaches temporal blessing to upright behavior.

When Kim Kyang Won, secretary general to South Korea's president, was asked about the reasons for his country's progress, he replied, "It's the culture of discipline and postponing immediate satisfaction for the future—even for posterity."[15] Such character traits have encouraged a national investment rate of 25 to 35 percent of the Gross National Product, twice the U.S. rate.

American evangelicals can learn from the Asian example of diligence and future-orientation. Being the "salt of the earth" in our own society implies such character traits. God's temporal blessing can then be directed not toward needless self-gratification, but toward financing the further expansion of the kingdom of God.

4

The Bible and Economic Equality

There appear to be a growing number of voices in Christian circles today calling for a massive redistribution of society's wealth. Jeremy Rifkin, author of *Entropy*, is concerned that today "the top one-fifth of the American population consumes over forty percent of the nation's wealth." Without a "fundamental redistribution of wealth," he believes, "all talk of lowering energy flow and heeding our planet's biological limits will result in nothing but the rich locking the poor forever into their subservient status."[1]

Jim Wallis, editor of *Sojourners* magazine, speaks of the "brutal disparities between rich and poor." According to Wallis, "the bottom fifth of American families get 6 percent of the national income while the top fifth get 40 percent of the national income, owns 77 percent of the wealth and 97 percent of the corporate stock."[2] Evidently Wallis believes that such differences in income distribution are in themselves immoral.

Similar concerns have been expressed by Dom Helder Camara, archbishop of Recife, Brazil. Speaking in a Latin American context, Camara notes that "the northern hemisphere, the developed area of the world, the 20 percent who possess 80 percent of the world's resources, are of Christian origin." Camara believes that the developed nations' wealth is the cause of the Third World's misery. "The 20 percent who are keeping the 80 percent in a situation which is often subhuman—are they or are they not," he asks, "responsible for the violence and hatred which are beginning to break out all over the world?"[3]

In his widely read book, *Rich Christians in an Age of Hunger*, Ron Sider says that God disapproves of great extremes of wealth and poverty. According to Sider, God created mechanisms and structures to prevent great economic inequality among his people.[4] One of these mechanisms, the Jubilee (Lev. 25), will be examined in this chapter.

Does the Bible encourage or even command a massive redistribution of the world's wealth? If Wallis, Camara, Sider, and others are correct, then it would appear that American Christians, simply by being Americans, are continually living in a state of sin. Before accepting such guilt-inducing claims, it is obviously important to ask whether such charges are biblically based.

Other significant questions arise in connection with calls for a redistribution of the world's wealth. What about "voluntary poverty" as a Christian lifestyle? Is there a biblical mandate for the Christian to adopt a minimal standard of living in order to give more to the poor?

How should our tax system be structured in order to promote social justice? Does the Bible necessarily favor a highly progressive tax system, which "soaks the rich" in order, presumably, to help the poor?

Does capitalism as an economic system inevitably create and perpetuate growing disparities between rich and poor? Should the Christian conclude, given biblical principles, that socialism is a morally superior economic system? These are some of the crucial questions concerning the distribution of wealth that call for a careful examination of the biblical data.

"Egalitarian" Texts in the Bible

One of the most important biblical texts in these recent discussions is found in Leviticus 25, which concerns the Year of Jubilee. Ron Sider has suggested that Christians celebrate a modern Jubilee, in which "all Christians worldwide would pool all their stocks, bonds, and income producing property and businesses and redistribute them equally. . . . There would undoubtedly be a certain amount of confusion and disruption. But then good things are seldom easy."[5]

According to the text of Leviticus 25, every 50 years the ancestral land grants were to revert to the original family owners. The land was not to be sold in perpetuity (v. 23). The original owner was to retain an option to repurchase the land on a prorated basis prior to the Jubilee (vv. 25-27). If a man had become too poor to repurchase the property, it was to revert to him without charge in the year of Jubilee (v. 28). A Hebrew slave was not to serve in perpetuity, but was to be released, together with his wife and children, during the fiftieth year (vv. 39-41). This release of slaves during the Jubilee year spiritually prefigured the release from the bondage of sin through the gospel (Luke 4:16-19; cf. Isa. 61:1-2; Lev. 25:39-41).

Now the question is, Does Leviticus 25 teach that Christians today should favor government policies that have as a specific purpose a general redistribution of income? While at first glance it might appear that way, a more careful reading of the provisions of Leviticus 25 will indicate otherwise.

First of all, the Jubilee legislation presupposes the *special covenant* and the *special revelation* given to Israel as a theocratic society (v. 1, "The Lord said to Moses on Mount Sinai"). The United States is not a theocratic society. It is generally agreed among conservative scholars that while the moral laws of the Old Testament are binding upon the New Testament church, the civil and ceremonial laws are not. The Jubilee legislation was part of the civil law of Israel. As we have already seen, the New Testament (Luke 4:16-19) indicates that the Old Testament Jubilee is spiritually fulfilled in the spiritual release from sin proclaimed in the gospel.

It is very important to notice that Leviticus 25 is not really concerned with *income equalization* but with the *restoration of leased family lands.* The Jubilee legislation said, in effect, that family lands could be leased for a maximum period of 49 years, but not sold in perpetuity (v. 23). While lands that had not been repurchased by the original owner on a prorated basis prior to the Jubilee reverted in any case during the fiftieth year, the *incomes* earned prior to the Jubilee were retained by the most recent owner. That is why it is more correct to say that the Jubilee legislation was concerned with limitations on the terms of leases rather than with general income redistribution. The fact is that nowhere in Leviticus 25 is it specified that income derived from use of the land is to be redistributed.

The provisions of Leviticus 25 were intended to safeguard equal *opportunity* for Israelites to earn income without destroying the *incentives* to work and invest through normal economic activities. Unlike many modern welfare programs and systems of progressive taxation, the Jubilee laws, by allowing retention of income earned from the land, did not destroy the incentives to work and invest, which are essential to the economic well-being of a society.

Notice also that Leviticus 25 is not a program of land "expropriation" or seizure as, for example, in the case of certain Latin American programs of "land reform." In the Jubilee laws, there is *compensation* for land restored to the original owner. In the case of land redeemed prior to the Jubilee, the most recent owner was compensated with a repurchase price calculated on a prorated basis. In the case of land reverting back to an impoverished original owner on the fiftieth year (v. 28), the most recent owner still had the compensation of retaining the income earned from the use of the property while the title was his. In neither case was it a matter of "robbing Peter to pay Paul," or of the government's acting in a Robin Hood fashion in the name of social justice. The eighth commandment, "You shall not steal," applies to governments as well as to individuals.

It is also significant that neither houses in walled cities (vv. 29, 30) nor foreign slaves (vv. 44-46) were included in the release provisions of the Jubilee legislation. This is yet another indication that Leviticus 25 is not concerned with general income redistribution, since both items represented forms of wealth. The houses in the walled cities, which did not revert, are more pertinent to our modern urban society than the agrarian properties, which did revert.

All this is not to say that Leviticus 25 has no significance for the structuring of modern society; that would be contrary to the spirit of New Testament texts such as Romans 15:4, which remind us that the entire Old Testament was written for our instruction. While a literal application of Leviticus 25 today seems neither possible nor appropriate, we can see in the text the very relevant social ideal of *equality of opportunity* for the members of a society. While this should not be misconstrued to mean a forced redistribution of income by the state, Christians can and should support policies that safeguard the *opportunities* of all to earn the incomes their efforts and abilities merit.

Three sets of texts in the New Testament call for attention in relation to equality of income as a purported biblical ideal. In the Gospel of John, it seems to be implied that the disciples shared a common purse (cf. 12:6; 13:29), which happened to be administered by Judas. Is such a common purse normative for the church today? Such a conclusion would overlook the special conditions presupposed by the text, i.e., the three-year itinerant ministry of Jesus and the Twelve prior to the crucifixion. While such a financial arrangement might still be appropriate for a missionary fellowship or monastic order, the more usual situation presupposed by the New Testament is the one where the believer is employed for income (II Thess. 3:12) and caring for members of the family (I Tim. 5:8).

Over the centuries many Christian groups have seen in the sharing of possessions by the Jerusalem church (Acts 2:44-47; 4:34-37) a continuing ideal for the later church. While Christian generosity to meet cases of urgent need in the fellowship is mandated by the New Testament (Gal. 6:10; James 2:15-17; I John 3:17), it is important to recognize the special historical circumstances that influenced the particular form this giving took in the Jerusalem church. This sharing of possessions in a "communistic" way was both *voluntary* and *temporary*. Members sold and shared their possessions voluntarily, not as a legalistic requirement, as the remarks of Peter to Ananias demonstrate: "After it was sold, was it not at your disposal?" (Acts 5:4). The arrangements were evidently temporary, since no further mention of such practices is made in the later chapters of Acts; and in the churches founded by Paul, it is presupposed that believers will be working for a living and providing for their own families (II Thess. 3:12; I Tim. 5:8).

David Chilton has drawn attention to some other special circumstances in the Jerusalem church.[6] On the day of Pentecost some 3,000 converts were added to the church, and 5,000 shortly thereafter (Acts 2:41; 4:4). Many of these converts were visitors from various parts of the Roman Empire, and stayed in Jerusalem to receive further instruction in the faith from the apostles (2:41-42). Their immediate needs were met through the generous sharing of the Jerusalem believers. The Jerusalem residents who were believers may have been further inclined to sell their property in light of the fact that Jesus had predicted that Jerusalem was shortly to be destroyed by divine judgment (Matt. 24; Mark 13; Luke 21). Why hang on to "condemned property"?

The third text in this connection is found in II Corinthians 8, where the apostle Paul encourages the Corinthians to give generously to the collection for the poor in the Jerusalem church. "As a matter of equality your abundance at the present time should supply their want, so that their abundance may supply your want, that there may be equality" (v. 14). The key question here is the meaning of the word "equality." Does this mean strict arithmetic equality of income in the church?

The text does not support that conclusion. In II Corinthians 8:13-15 Paul is not saying that the incomes of the Corinthian and Jerusalem churches must be arithmetically equal, but that the generosity of the Corinthians should "supply their want" (v. 14), i.e., their case of urgent need. This is precisely the force of similar passages in the New Testament (for example, I Timothy 6:17-19) which presuppose differences of income in the church. The New Testament scholar J. H. Bernard observes in *The Expositor's Greek Testament* that the word translated "equality" has the sense of "reciprocity": "What is meant is that if it ever came to the turn of Corinth to be poor, then it would be for Jerusalem to contribute for her support."[7]

The word for "equality" occurs in only one other passage in the

New Testament, Colossians 4:1, where Paul commands masters to. give justice and "fairness" to their slaves. Here equality or fairness is not sameness of income, but the necessities of life and humane treatment, "what is necessary for the body" (James 2:16).

Voluntary Poverty, Taxation, Capitalism, and Inequality

One issue that arises in connection with the ideal of economic equality is "voluntary poverty." Walt and Ginny Hearn, writing in the *Post American*, affirmed their belief that "deliberately lowering our standard of living in obedience to God is part of what Jesus meant by being 'poor in spirit.' " Since they have voluntarily lowered their expenditures, they have found, they say, "that the quality of our life seems higher than before."[8]

Such an ideal of "simple living," freeing more income to give to the work of the kingdom, has considerable appeal in the Christian community today, especially among the young. Other reasons given by the Hearns for their decision to adopt such a lifestyle are that "it may be the only way to sustain religious revival"; that it is an "ecological imperative"; that "it makes possible alternative [low paid] vocations of social significance"; that it "builds constructive human relationships by making us dependent on each other."

Without question there are many admirable elements in the ideal of "voluntary poverty." It has deep roots in the Christian tradition, reaching back to the monastic movements of the early church and Middle Ages. It seems undeniable that the "voluntary poverty" ideal reflects basic teachings in the Scriptures such as the command to seek first the kingdom of God (Matt. 6:33), to be wary of all covetousness and greed, since life does not consist in the abundance of possessions (Luke 12:15), and to remember that the things that are seen are transient, but the things that are unseen are eternal (II Cor. 4:18).

At the same time, spiritual dangers can arise when such an outlook is carried too far. Those who pursue the ideal of voluntary poverty run the risk of legalism and spiritual pride. The mentality that says, in effect, "You *must* live at the poverty level in order to be a serious disciple of Jesus," represents a legalistic distortion of the gospel. The apostle Paul exhorted the wealthy to be generous (I Tim. 6:18), but he did not "read them out of the church" merely because of their wealth.

Spiritual pride, it is said, is the most subtle of all the sins. In the pursuit of a legitimate ideal such as voluntary poverty the believer needs to be wary of falling into a "poorer than thou" mentality. Our righteousness in God's sight is always found in Jesus Christ—not in our outward circumstances, whether wealth or poverty. "If I give away all I have, and if I deliver my body to be burned, but have not love, I gain nothing" (I Cor. 13:3).

There is also the curious irony that taking the "simple living" ideal to an extreme can actually make our life more complicated. An excessive reaction to "materialism" can lead us to become pre-occupied with material things. If I would need to spend an entire day searching for a part in automotive junkyards in order to save $20, it might be better stewardship of my time and resources to pay full price for the part, and spend my time in activities that are more directly people-related.

The "voluntary poverty" ideal should not be taken to such an extreme that we can no longer enjoy the goodness and abundance of God's world. "Everything created by God is good, and nothing is to be rejected if it is received with thanksgiving" (I Tim. 4:4). Paul certainly knew how to be abased, but he also knew how to enjoy abundance, when God provided such (Phil. 4:12).

Those who are considering the voluntary poverty option should carefully weigh the pros and cons. While decreasing expenditures can free more money for kingdom giving, in the long run, consistent *tithing* of a *growing* income can produce even more resources for the kingdom of God. The merits of an "ethic of conservation" should be weighed against the merits of an "ethic of production." If an obedient Christian community tithed consistently from an expanding financial base, the effect on both church and society would be enormous.

Discussions of economic equality inevitably raise questions about taxation. As a purely practical matter, those serious about implementing economic equality look to the tax system as a primary means of redistributing society's wealth. We have already seen that the arguments from Scripture in favor of economic egalitarianism are weak. What about the practical effects of highly progressive systems of taxation designed to "soak the rich" in the name of social justice? Does recent experience show that such schemes provide a better life for society as a whole?

Before looking at the postwar experience of England and the United States, a bit of historical perspective is necessary. Most Americans have become so accustomed to relatively high rates of taxation that they hardly realize that things were much different earlier in our nation's history. Dr. Gary North, a conservative Christian economist writing in the *Remnant Review,* points out that prior to World War I, the entire national debt was about $1.2 billion. In 1897 the entire tax collections of the federal government was $146 million. And of that incredibly low figure, some $114 million, or 78 percent of the total, was derived from excise taxes on alcohol. Dr. North comments that the federal government was financed largely by people who were "feeling no pain" anyway. The remainder of the federal income was derived from excise taxes on tobacco, stamp taxes, and excise taxes on manufactures.[9] In what now seems like the dim and distant past, the federal government was financed with no income tax at all. A key factor in the equation was, of course, that people expected fewer services from government. As a result, government was a much lighter burden to the taxpayers.

The postwar experience of England has demonstrated the folly and futility of progressive taxation. For decades British domestic policy has focused on a drive for greater equality of income. "Measure after measure has been adopted designed to take from the rich and give to the poor," observes Professor Milton Friedman. Taxes on income were raised to a maximum of 98 percent on property income and 83 percent on "earned" income, together with heavy taxes on inheritances.[10]

Rather than creating a truly egalitarian society, Britain's tax laws have created new elites: the tenured government bureaucrats; the trade unions, which represent the aristocracy of the labor movement; and new millionaires who have been clever enough to find loopholes in the laws.

By ignoring one of the most fundamental aspects of human nature, namely the desire to benefit from the fruits of one's efforts, Britain's tax laws have helped to create a "brain drain" depriving the country of some of its most energetic and talented citizens. Tax laws that have stifled incentives to work and invest are primary contributors to lagging British productivity—far behind its European neighbors, the United States, and Japan.

A similar tax situation has applied in postwar America. George Gilder, writing in 1981, pointed out that the top 1 percent of America's income earners were paying nearly 20 percent of the federal income taxes, and the top 25 percent were paying 72 percent.[11] This represented a highly "progressive" philosophy of taxation. The United States, Gilder pointed out, was taxing capital gains and assets at rates eight times higher than Sweden and about four times higher than Germany or Japan.[12]

During the last several years it has become increasingly clear that American tax policies have discouraged the degree of savings and investment necessary to create new jobs and increase productivity. "Steeply progressive rates may have an idealistic ring," noted Gilder, "but their effect is to reduce incentives for economic success, work, and risk."[13] Lagging American productivity has demonstrated that punitive attitudes toward wealth and its creation in the long run only serve to make society as a whole less prosperous. The Reagan Administration's tax cuts of 1981 were a response to a growing perception of these realities among the nation as a whole.

A final matter in relation to the ideal of economic equality concerns the nature of the free enterprise system itself. Does capitalism inevitably lead to greater and greater inequalities in a society? The belief that it does has led many intellectuals to endorse socialism as a presumably more just and humane economic system.

The facts, however, point to a different conclusion. As Professor Friedman has pointed out, "Nowhere is the gap between rich and poor wider, nowhere are the rich richer and the poor poorer, than in those societies that do not permit the free market to operate."[14] This has been demonstrated in the experience of medieval Europe, and today in India, much of South America, China, and the Soviet Union. Asian states, on the other hand, such as South Korea, Taiwan, Singapore, and Hong Kong, oriented toward the free market, have exhibited both economic prosperity and tremendous opportunities for industrious individuals to improve their economic conditions.

Marxist societies have long claimed that their "egalitarianism" is a badge of moral superiority in relation to the "class societies" produced by capitalism. The alleged egalitarianism of Communist states tends to disappear under closer examination.

There have been protests in Poland about the luxurious vacation resorts for Communist Party members, about the special coupons that allow party officials to buy the best food without waiting in the lines created by their system, and about the prevalence of "Bermudas"—the luxury housing developments where the elite live in relative seclusion. The head of Polish Radio and Television, notes Daniel Seligman, writing in *Fortune*, "was found to have owned a 40-acre farm, a 5-room villa with a glass-bottomed swimming pool, another residence described as a palace, and a yacht."[15]

Mervyn Matthews, in his book *Privilege in the Soviet Union*, has described in detail the intricate arrangements that make it possible for a society presumably founded on egalitarianism to provide its elite with luxury housing, live-in maids, chauffeured limousines, special stores, special vacation resorts, special travel privileges—from all of which the average citizen is excluded.[16] The facts disclosed by Matthews and others demonstrate that the barriers of class, power, and privilege are far higher in countries controlled by Communist parties than they are in nations where the free market is allowed to operate.

The constant stream of refugees flowing toward the United States and away from the Communist nations demonstrates that the greater personal freedoms and opportunities in a free enterprise system are not some idle dream concocted by conservative intellectuals. Countless millions have, as the saying goes, "voted for the system with their feet."

Eric Hoffer, the self-educated longshoreman and philosopher, expresses the point fittingly: "I have been poor most of my life," confessed Hoffer, "and in my years as a migratory worker I was often but a step ahead of hunger. Yet it never occurred to me that there could be a country where I would be more at ease or more at home. . . . That is what millions of immigrants who came to this country also looked for: a chance to do what they wanted to do. Many failed, but there were more chances here than anywhere else.[17]

5

The Government's Role in Alleviating Poverty

Some time ago, in an article in *New York* magazine, the well-known liberal economist John Kenneth Galbraith was quoted as saying, "I have no doubt that nearly all of the problems of New York could be solved by the simple device of spending enough money."[1] Whether or not Professor Galbraith has since revised his opinion in the light of recent experience, it seems clear that great numbers of Americans now question the validity of the once-dominant liberal philosophy of "throwing money at the problem" in order to cure social ills.

Liberal leaders are now groping for new ideas and directions. "The greatest problem we confront is that we are called liberals," said former Representative Elizabeth Holtzman of New York in a keynote address at a recent convention of the Americans for Democratic Action. "Frankly, liberalism has come to mean something pejorative over the past few years," Ms. Holtzman stated. "It is associated with give-aways, with a prodigal, prolific public spending of people's hard-earned tax dollars."[2]

If the 1980 fall elections were any indication, then evidently many Americans agreed with Ms. Holtzman's analysis. There is unquestionably a healthy debate going on today both outside the church and within it about the role of government in alleviating poverty and other social problems. Should government maintain the activist posture taken since the days of the New Deal, or should it lower its profile in deference to the private sector? What lessons can be learned from Scripture and from the experience of other nations? To what extent have government welfare programs in the last several decades achieved their stated goals? These are some of the important questions to be addressed in this chapter.

Insights from Scripture

Since much biblical data has already been discussed in the chapter on poverty, we need only recall some of that here. As we noted, Old Testament law permitted needy persons to pick and eat from a neighbor's field in order to meet cases of urgent need (Deut. 23: 24, 25). The privilege was not to be abused, however. The use of a vessel or a sickle, which implied intent to take more than immediate needs required, was expressly forbidden (vv. 24b, 25h). The poor were also allowed to glean from the fields at harvest time (Lev. 19:9, 10; 23:22; Deut. 24:19-21). Every seventh year the land was to be left fallow, and the poor and sojourner were to be allowed to eat from what grew of itself (Lev. 25:4-7). On the fiftieth year, the year of Jubilee, the land was again to lie fallow, and each family was to return to its ancestral property (vv. 8-34).

A number of comments are in order concerning these provisions of Old Testament law. They clearly express God's concern for the poor and needy. At the same time, there are significant differences between these biblical laws and some of our modern solutions to similar problems. In the first place, these Old Testament laws presuppose a limited involvement on the part of the central government. The Mosaic provisions place a "safety net" under the poor, but do not represent any attempt at a wholesale redistribution of income or general restructuring of society. These provisions created no administrative bureaucracies. On the contrary, the aid passed rather directly from, for example, the owner of a field to the needy gleaner. Such a small-scale transfer at the local level avoided the impersonality of modern transfer payments through taxation. The owner of the field would be in a position literally to "meet the need" as a living person, and not merely as a statistic.

The Mosaic provisions, unlike some modern welfare programs, did not reduce or remove the incentives to work. The gleaner was required to exert some effort; under normal circumstances, it was much simpler to earn one's daily bread through the more usual forms of employment.

It is also worth noting that the Mosaic provisions concerning the poor operated through moral suasion. Generosity to the poor was commanded, but that was to be a willing response to the grace of God. Unlike other parts of Old Testament law, violations of these provisions were not sanctioned by fines, beatings, or capital penalties. In both testaments it is true that "God loves a cheerful giver." Modern welfare programs financed by compulsory taxation—and backed by the coercive power of the criminal law—actually tend to dry up the wellsprings of charity freely given.

While neither the Old nor the New Testament articulates detailed theories concerning the proper scope and functions of the state, both testaments point to the wisdom of a limited government philosophy. In I Samuel 8, the prophet Samuel warns the people about the dangers of kingship, and assumes that even a 10 percent level of taxation (v. 15) represents an oppressive burden. In Romans 13, a key text on the Christian's attitude toward the state, the principal functions of the magistrate appear to be judicial and military in nature. As the bearer of the sword (v. 4) the magistrate is to punish domestic criminals and protect the people from foreign aggressors. Paul does not comment on the purposes for which taxes (vv. 6,7) should be used, but given his Old Testament heritage as a Jew, he undoubtedly would have seen the primary responsibility for poor relief to be in the private sector.

While Romans 13 is usually discussed in relation to questions of government, Revelation 13 is frequently overlooked. In this vision the prophet John sees a "beast rising out of the sea," a symbolic depiction of the Roman Empire. This empire, representing the greatest concentration of political and economic power in history to that date, was waging war against the Christian church. Verse 17 alludes to the concentrated economic power of the empire: "No one can buy or sell unless he has the mark, that is, the name of the beast or the number of its name." History has shown that states exhibiting great concentrations of economic and political power in the hands of elite groups all too often attack the religious liberties of their people. The experience of Christians and Jews in the Soviet Union is a recent case in point. The pride and arrogance of too much power can corrupt a government. The Christians of the Roman Empire were persecuted by a beast "uttering haughty and blasphemous words" (v. 5).

As we have already noted in chapter one, the Founding Fathers, influenced by both the Judeo-Christian tradition of the Bible, and their recollections of the tyrannies of European history, believed in a philosophy of limited government. The checks and balances written into the Constitution reflect a belief in the fallenness of human nature and the inevitable tendency of concentrated power to corrupt.

The powers of government were to be strictly controlled. George Washington affirmed that government ". . . is not reason, it is not eloquence—it is force. Like fire it is a dangerous servant and a fearful master; never for a moment should it be left to irresponsible action."[3] In his First Inaugural Address, Thomas Jefferson declared that a "wise and frugal government," which would restrain the citizens from injuring one another, would "leave them otherwise free to regulate their own pursuits of industry and improvement, and shall not take from the mouth of labor the bread it has earned."[4] Washington and Jefferson would no doubt be astonished to discover the extent to which our government today, in the name of social justice and compassion, has intruded itself in the private affairs of its citizens and is taking "from the mouth of labor the bread it has earned."

Some Lessons from History

The history of certain government-sponsored welfare programs is most instructive. H. J. Haskell, in his book *The New Deal in Ancient Rome*, described that ancient city's welfare system. There was no income test; anyone who was willing to stand in the bread lines could take advantage of the subsidized prices. Some 50,000 applied initially, but the numbers kept increasing with time. A politician named Claudius ran for the office of tribune on a free-wheat platform and was elected. A decade later, when Julius Caesar had come to power, there were some 320,000 people on the government grain dole. Under the emperor Aurelian the dole was made a hereditary right. Two pounds of bread were distributed daily to all registered citizens who applied, and pork, olive oil, and salt were also given without charge at periodic intervals.[5]

Such a welfare system had predictable effects on Roman character and work habits. As Henry Hazlitt has observed, the system "undermined the old Roman virtues of self-reliance. It schooled people to expect something for nothing." The system was financed by increasingly burdensome taxes that helped to strangle the Roman economy.[6]

England was among the first modern Western nations to experiment with an extensive program of public relief. The total expenditures for the program in 1785 was about £2 million; by 1803 it had increased to approximately £4 million; and by 1817 it had reached almost £8 million. In this case the "supply" of welfare created a demand for such services that appeared to increase at a geometric rate.

The rapidly ballooning costs and reported abuses led the government to appoint a Royal commission to investigate the matter. The 1834 report of the commission stated some sobering conclusions, which are still timely almost a century and a half later: "The laborer under the existing system," noted the commission, "need not bestir himself to seek work; he need not study to please his master; he need not put any restraint upon his temper. . . . He has all a slave's security for subsistence, without his liability to punishment."

The commission's report pointed to the adverse effects of the system on the incentive to work: "Every penny bestowed, that tends to render the condition of the pauper more eligible than that of the independent laborer, is a bounty on indolence and vice." In a somewhat prophetic note the commission concluded, "We do not believe that a country in which . . . every man whatever his conduct or character is insured a comfortable subsistence, can retain its prosperity, or even its civilization."[7] The Royal Commissioners, had they the ability through some time machine to visit the modern British welfare state, now widely known abroad for its economic doldrums, urban riots, and punk rock, might well conclude that their views had been vindicated.

Recent American Experience

In recent years there has been an increasing sense of dissatisfaction with government programs meant to solve the problems of the poor in America. Some such dissatisfaction comes from leaders within the black community. Arthur Ashe, the famous tennis player, has stated, "Black people have to stop depending on the government—federal, state, and city—as their savior. We're starting to get the tools. Now we must go out and do it ourselves. . . . If you have ability, you can find a job."[8]

Ashe is not the only black spokesman to voice a new appreciation for the free enterprise system. Thomas Sowell, the highly respected black economist at Stanford University, has declared that his people have "had enough social experiments with blacks as guinea pigs. We want to enlarge the opportunities for black people to solve their own problems."[9] Sowell has been instrumental in founding a new black organization intended to provide a conservative alternative to more liberally oriented groups such as the NAACP and the Urban League.

Reasons for the growing dissatisfaction with government intervention are not hard to find. The federally mandated minimum wage law is a good case in point. While the original impetus for such laws came from the labor unions, many intellectuals supported the policy in the belief that such laws would help alleviate the condition of the poor. This belief has not been sustained by actual experience. After the minimum wage was raised sharply, unemployment rates for both black and white teenagers, but especially black teenagers, rose dramatically. The unemployment rate for white teenagers is approximately 15 to 20 percent, and 35 to 45 percent for black teenagers, creating a highly explosive social situation.[10] By creating artificially high wage rates, the laws effectively discriminate against unskilled black teenagers and price them out of the labor market. Milton Friedman regards the minimum wage law as "one of the most, if not the most, antiblack laws on the statute books."[11] Such laws were advocated as being in the interest of the poor, but in actuality, they only serve to benefit the unions by creating higher wage floors for their members. The minimum wage law is a prime example of how a federal policy can actually contribute to a social problem it was enacted to solve.

Another federal program whose public image has become considerably tarnished in recent years is CETA, the "Comprehensive Employment and Training Act." The original aims of CETA were laudable ones, namely to provide training and job opportunities for those unable to find employment. While there is no question that some people have been helped, CETA programs all too often have been characterized by frivolity and waste.

A Chicago CETA program paid a young employee $750 a month to teach ghetto youth how to slap various parts of their bodies rhythmically in order to become "human drums." In order to provide a practice facility for rock-climbers, a CETA agency in Salem, Oregon, financed the construction of a steel-reinforced concrete rock 30 feet high and 60 feet across on a small island in the Willamette River. In Ventura, California, a CETA agency paid 101 people to count the dogs, cats, and horses in the county.[12]

According to a report issued by the General Accounting Office, it costs about $20,000 to create a job through the CETA program—perhaps twice as much as the cost of the creation of a similar job by a small business. By siphoning revenues from the private sector, the total effect of the CETA program may well be actually to lower the level of employment.[13]

There is not only the issue of waste and frivolity—e.g., the $500,000 spent to train people to deal blackjack, spin roulette wheels, and run crap tables in the casinos of Atlantic City, New Jersey[14]—but also the matter of the more subtle effects on the character and outlook of the people involved in such programs. The problem with such make-work schemes, according to George Gilder, is that, like welfare, "CETA often has the effect of shielding people from the realities of their lives and thus prevents them from growing up and finding or creating useful tasks."[15] Lacking the full discipline of the marketplace, such programs can obscure the distinction between work and play, and actually delay the perhaps painful personal reorientation necessary to function successfully in the real world.

Criticism of the government's attempts to alleviate poverty has focused, of course, on the welfare system. One aspect of the welfare problem that might be overlooked in the midst of other criticisms concerns the dramatic postwar growth of government welfare programs as a whole. While total wages and salaries during the years 1945–1979 grew at an average annual rate of 7.1 percent, government transfer payments grew at an annual rate of 11.5 percent.[16] The welfare establishment thus represented one of the major "growth industries" in postwar America. By 1980, 44 different welfare programs were consuming more than $200 billion—more than the entire federal budget in 1973.[17] In practical terms, this meant an increasingly heavy burden for the average taxpayer. Today, government consumes over 35 percent of all goods and services produced.[18] It is little wonder that cries of "tax revolt" are being heard around the land.

Outright fraud in government welfare programs has helped to tarnish the image of such programs in the eyes of many. Over a six-year period a woman in Los Angeles collected $240,000 in welfare, claiming 66 nonexistent children, before she was apprehended by authorities. A graduate student in Chicago collected $150,000 in illegal payments from 1972 through 1978.[19]

According to city comptroller Harrison Golden, thousands of dead New Yorkers were being mailed millions of dollars in government social program payments and medical benefits for up to 20 months after their deaths. "This condition exists throughout New York State and may be costing the federal, state, and local governments $11 million per year," Golden said. One man who died on March 16, 1979, was paid for five methadone clinic visits supposedly made from May 21 to May 25 of that year. In one case, a family received public assistance benefits for seven months after a family member died.[20]

Justice Department officials have testified that money lost through fraud and waste could amount to as much as ten percent of the total spending for federal assistance programs.[21] The Department of Health and Human Services (formerly HEW) estimated that it lost in fiscal 1979 $2 *billion* in overpayments or payments to ineligible parties. Officials say they hope to reduce this "slippage" to four percent—but that would still represent $1.1 billion in overpayments.[22]

Auditors uncovered a glaring example of mismanagement in the Social Security Administration. The auditors estimated that the Social Security fund was losing approximately $4.5 million a year in interest on money withdrawn before it was actually needed to pay benefits.[23]

Examples of waste and inefficiency are not limited to the Department of Health and Human Services. Auditors discovered that virtually half of a $100,000 Office of Minority Business Enterprise grant to a southern Illinois company had been squandered on unjustified salaries, travel, and parties. By the time congressional investigators reviewed the case, the company had gone out of business.[24]

At boarding schools in Oklahoma operated by the Bureau of Indian Affairs, year-end spending sprees have pushed per-pupil costs as high as $10,281 a year. One school with an enrollment of 168 purchased 4 hair dryers, 5 electric typewriters, and 2 popcorn machines, even though it already had popcorn machines in every dormitory, unused hair dryers in storage, and 14 typewriters for 4 typists.[25]

Officials of the Department of Housing and Urban Development (HUD) guaranteed the mortgage for a 240-space trailer park in Royce City, Texas (pop. 1800) without a careful determination of need. When after 2 years the park did not have a single occupant, HUD foreclosed and auctioned off the $765,000 project for $51,000. The loss was absorbed by the taxpayers.[26]

Such examples of waste and poor management in government programs could be multiplied almost endlessly. The frequency of such bungling reflects the basic fact that government bureaucrats are, unlike those operating businesses in the private sector, shielded from the discipline of the marketplace. If a government welfare agency is guilty of mismanagement, the taxpayers are always there to pick up the tab. Such programs lack the hard *accountability* that characterizes the private sector. Federal agencies, which spend *other people's money*, lack the incentives for thrift and efficiency that characterize private businesses, which must account for their own mistakes.

One of the persistent criticisms of government welfare programs has been that they tend to benefit the bureaucrats who administer them more than the poor they were presumably created to serve. This is being admitted even by once-ardent advocates of such programs. Elizabeth Holtzman, the former Democratic House member from New York, noted that some of the poverty programs created by liberals over the past two decades "became vehicles for enriching the people who administered them, instead of the people they were intended for." During the elections of 1980, she noted, "Liberalism was viewed as a defense of the status quo, of social programs that didn't work and that were wasteful."[27]

Professor Thomas Sowell of Stanford has pointed out that the amount of money necessary to lift every man, woman, and child in America above the poverty line is *one-third* of what in fact is being spent on poverty programs. "Clearly," he notes, "much of the transfer ends up in the pockets of highly paid administrators, consultants, and staff, as well as higher-income recipients of benefits from programs advertised as anti-poverty efforts."[28]

Even more distressing, from a Christian point of view, than all the examples of waste and mismanagement is the negative impact many welfare programs have had upon poor families. In many cases well-intended but misguided programs have actually given ghetto fathers financial incentives to leave their families. In such cases the ghetto male has discovered that welfare payments to a "single" mother are greater than what he can earn through legitimate employment. Such programs have the effect of emasculating ghetto males. As a result, notes George Gilder, "boys are brought up without authoritative fathers in the home to instill in them the values of responsible paternity: the discipline and love of children and the dependable performance of the provider role."[29] Ill-conceived welfare programs can thus inadvertently contribute to the level of antisocial and criminal behavior in the ghetto.

Welfare programs can have other corrupting effects on those involved in them. By putting some people (the administrators) in a position to decide what is good for other people, such programs can instill in the one group a feeling of almost "God-like power," as Milton Friedman has put it. The beneficiaries are placed in a position of childlike dependence, and the capacity for independence and initiative tends to atrophy through disuse. The end result, according to Friedman, "is to rot the moral fabric that holds a decent society together."[30] The basic problem with welfare, George Gilder has observed, is that it now "erodes work and family and thus keeps poor people poor."[31]

Such criticisms of government welfare programs are achieving widespread circulation today. The question of alternatives naturally arises. Can the private sector do a better job? Can private charity really meet the needs of the poor? What is the proper role of the church in alleviating poverty? Such questions will be addressed in the following chapter.

6

The Church's Role in Alleviating Poverty

"In a local community in their country a citizen may conceive of some need that is not being met. . . . A committee comes into existence and then the committee begins functioning on behalf of that need. . . . All this is done without reference to any bureaucrat. All this is done by the private citizens on their own initiative." Thus spoke the Frenchman Alexis de Tocqueville on his visit to America in 1830. De Tocqueville was impressed by the American spirit, which was characterized by private initiative rather than dependence on governmental bureaucracy. "The health of a democratic society," he observed, "may be measured by the quality of functions performed by private citizens."[1]

The spirit of voluntarism is still alive today. It has been estimated that there are some 500,000 organized philanthropic and civic groups in the United States.[2] Americans support nearly 80 percent of the world's private charities.[3] And yet the question arises, can purely voluntary efforts deal adequately with social problems such as poverty? Hasn't history shown that only the resources of government are extensive enough to meet such problems? What is the role of the church as a private organization in the alleviation of poverty? What does the Bible teach concerning the church's ministry to those

61

with temporal needs? These are some of the issues to be explored in this chapter.

Approaches That Haven't Worked

If de Tocqueville were to visit America today, he would surely be astounded at the massive growth of government in relation to the private sector. Prior to 1935 and the days of the New Deal, over 50 percent of all welfare spending was in the private sector; today it is about 1 percent.[4] The massive growth of government involvement in American life can be traced in the rising levels of government spending. Except for major wars, government spending from 1800 to 1929 did not exceed approximately 12 percent of the national income, and two-thirds of that was spent by state and local governments, mostly for schools and roads. "As late as 1928," Milton Friedman has observed, "federal government spending amounted to about 3 percent of the national income."[5]

As we have noted in previous chapters, there is in America today a growing sense of dissatisfaction with government-mandated transfer programs as solutions to the nation's welfare problem. But should Christians not be concerned with poverty? Is the God of the Bible not concerned with the poor? "Of course the Christian must be concerned—indeed the most concerned of all for the poor," replies the conservative theologian R. C. Sproul. "But the Christian should be the last to embrace statism as a societal goal—he should be the last to sanction political force as a means of economic redistribution." The Bible alerts us to the problem of poverty, but does not endorse a "Robin Hood" philosophy as the solution for it. "In every experiment in world history of forceful redistribution of a people's wealth," observes Sproul, "the bottom line was a *lowering* of the people's standard of living."[6]

As we have noted, recent government transfer programs and concepts, such as "Affirmative Action," have, in the name of social justice, transformed the American ideal of equality of *opportunity* into one of equality of *result*. We must not only leave the starting line at the same time, but also be awarded the same prizes, no matter who really finishes first. The meaning of the term "equality" has been thoroughly confused in the process. "When we speak of 'equal justice under the law,' we simply mean applying the same rules to everybody," writes Thomas Sowell of Stanford. "A good umpire calls balls and strikes by the same rules for everyone, but one batter may get twice as many hits as another."[7] It is a fallacy to conclude that if incomes differ, then the "system" *must* be rigged. In some cases, of course, it could be, but in other cases, unequal results may reflect unequal individual skills and effort.

We have also seen that a prime source of dissatisfaction with many government welfare programs is the perception that the major beneficiaries of such programs are the employees of government itself. M. Stanton Evans notes in his book *Clear and Present Dangers* the growing perception that such programs "transfer money away from relatively low income people—average taxpayers who must pay the bills—to relatively high income people—federal functionaries who are being paid out of the taxpayer's pocket." Is it simply accidental, Evans asks, that the two counties in the United States with the highest per capita income—Montgomery County, Maryland, and Fairfax County, Virginia—are the principal bedroom counties for federal workers in Washington, D.C.?[8] As Dr. Ronald Nash has remarked, "It pays to serve the poor under the aegis of the liberal state."[9]

The Church's Social Responsibility

It is not difficult today to recognize that government is no panacea for the problem of poverty. It is not so easy, however, to define the church's proper role in the matter. For this we need to turn to the guidance of Scripture.

The teachings of the Bible have been enormously influential over the centuries in promoting countless works of philanthropy and benevolence. As the successful Christian businessman Arnaud Marts has noted, "The Judaeo-Christian religion, throughout its centuries of development, has been the world's greatest teacher of justice and mercy, of the laws of God and of his love for all men.

Philanthropy—the love of mankind—is its natural fruitage."[10]

Christian concern for the temporal needs of man is rooted in such basic biblical doctrines as the creation of man, the incarnation of Jesus Christ, and the resurrection of the body. Man was not created by God as a disembodied soul, but as a psychosomatic whole of soul and body (Gen. 2:7). Salvation in Scripture is not liberation *from* the body—as in Platonic thought and much Eastern religion—but salvation of the whole person, body and soul. For the sake of our salvation, the Word was made *flesh* (John 1:14)—the Son of God assuming our true and entire human nature, while at the same time retaining his divine essence. The Christian hope beyond this life is for the resurrection of the *body*, not merely for the immortality of the soul. God made us as whole persons, redeemed us as whole persons, cares for us as whole persons, and will finally glorify us as whole persons.

The earthly ministry of Jesus demonstrated God's concern for the poor and needy. His primary mission was to die for the sins of many (Mark 10:45), but he demonstrated God's mercy and compassion by healing the sick, casting out demons, and feeding the five thousand. He taught his disciples to love their enemies (Matt. 5:44), an extension of the second great commandment of the Old Testament, to love our neighbors as ourselves (Lev. 19:18). Love in this context is not essentially a feeling, but concrete acts that meet a person's need.

Christ's entire ministry could be characterized as a life dedicated to serving the true needs of men and women. Peter could summarize that ministry in his sermon to Cornelius by saying that Jesus "went about doing good and healing all that were oppressed by the devil, for God was with him" (Acts 10:38).

The teachings of the apostles consistently command Christian concern for the poor and needy. We are to "do good to all men, especially to those who are of the household of faith" (Gal. 4:28). We are not to return evil for evil, but to seek to do good to all (I Thess. 5:15). Wealthy Christians are instructed to do good, to be rich in good deeds, and to be liberal and generous (I Tim. 6:18). Christians are to be zealous for good deeds (Titus 2:14; 3:8). The writer of Hebrews reminds the church to show hospitality to strangers and to remember those who are in prison and ill-treated (Heb. 13:2,3). James teaches that genuine faith is demonstrated in works that provide for a needy Christian brother or sister (James 2:14-17). John warns that if we close our hearts against a needy brother, the love of God does not truly abide in us (I John 3:17).

The Early Church and Middle Ages

"Richly was the word of our Lord fulfilled: 'By this shall all men know that you are my disciples, if you have love for one another.' . . . With amazement they [pagans] gazed upon this new life of love, and it is not too much to say that the victory of the church, like that of her Lord, was a victory of ministering love."[11] This conclusion of Gerhard Uhlhorn in his study, *The Conflict of Christianity with Heathenism,* is well supported by the facts of early church history. The church earned its right to be heard in a decadent Roman Empire through its compassionate ministry to the poor and distressed.

"They love each other without knowing each other," one pagan said of the Christians. Such brotherly love was not confined to the church, however. Justin Martyr, a church father of the second century, explained it this way: "Our religion requires us to love not only our own, but also strangers and even those who hate us."[12] Such a religion was a striking contrast to the egoistic philosophy voiced by the Roman writer Plautus: "A man is a wolf to a man whom he does not know."

In the pre-Christian Roman Empire, hospitals existed only for soldiers, gladiators, and slaves. Manual laborers and other poor individuals had no place of refuge. Men feared death, and took little interest in the sick, but often drove them out of the house, and left them to their fate.

At Alexandria, Egypt, during a pestilence in the time of the emperor Gallienus (*c.* 260), while the heathen fled and left the dying in the streets, the Christians cared not only for their own, but for the pagans as well. Many presbyters and deacons lost their lives in this sacrificial service. And, notes Uhlhorn, "they did this immediately after they had been most horribly persecuted by the heathen, and while the sword still hung daily over their heads."[13]

The early church gave financial aid to the poor; cared for widows and destitute orphans; rescued abandoned infants from the city dumps; gave Christian education to abandoned children, and visited the sick and the imprisoned. At the time of the Decian (*c.* 249) the church at Rome was supporting 1,500 poor persons, widows, and children. The boys were taught a trade, and all who could were required to work. Still later, the church in Antioch supported 3,000 beneficiaries.

The church father Tertullian could declare without exaggeration to the pagans, "Our compassion gives more in the streets than your religion in the temples." With the progressive decay of the old Roman order, the church was destined to become the major philanthropic organization in the civilized world.

During the Middle Ages the Christian church continued to be the almost exclusive promoter of charity and relief for the poor and suffering. The first documented record of a hospital is of one established at Caesarea in the year 369 by Saint Basil. It appears to have been a very extensive facility, with pavilions for various diseases, and residences for physicians, nurses, and convalescents.

After the Crusades, the number of hospitals multiplied at a remarkable rate throughout Europe and England. The church sponsored literally thousands of hospitals for lepers alone.[14]

The spirit and influence of Christian charity in the Middle Ages has been summed up by W. E. H. Lecky in his *History of European Morals:* "All through the darkest period . . . amid ferocity and fanaticism and brutality, we may trace the subduing influence of Catholic charity."[15] It was countless acts of Christian charity, perhaps as much as any other influence, that slowly turned the pagan tribes of Europe from barbarism toward the Christian faith.

The Evangelical Heritage

Evangelical Protestants have a long and glorious heritage of involvement in the problems of the poor and the needy. Much of this heritage, unfortunately, was forgotten in the wake of the modernist-fundamentalist controversy of the 1920s. As the evangelical historian Robert D. Linder has observed, in the years after 1925 "it became the habit to separate evangelism from social concern and to emphasize the individual and private at the expense of the corporate and public aspects of Christianity."[16] Social concern was viewed with suspicion because of its association with the "social gospel" and theological liberalism.

The nineteenth century was the great century of evangelical social concern, both in England and the United States. In England, William Wilberforce and his evangelical friends in the Clapham sect led a long but successful struggle for the abolition of the slave trade in the British Empire. Other evangelical leaders such as Anthony Ashley, the seventh Earl of Shaftsbury, and his friends Richard Oestler and Michael Sadler, worked to bring reform in the areas of child labor, treatment of the mentally ill, and housing for the poor. Men such as George Mueller and Charles H. Spurgeon expressed their evangelical concern in supporting orphanages for the poor. The development of Braille script for the blind, the founding of the Y.M.C.A. (1844), the Y.W.C.A. (1877), and the Red Cross were all part of the outflowing of evangelical social concern in nineteenth-century England.

In nineteenth-century America a wave of revivals produced a massive outpouring of evangelical philanthropic activity. Philip Schaff, the prominent church historian, observed in 1854, "There are in America probably more awakened souls and more individual self-sacrifice for religious purposes, proportionately, than in any other country in the world."[17]

The spiritual renewal produced by the revivals made the voluntary system work. By the years 1830–31, the 13 leading philanthropic societies had gathered $2,813,000. This figure, which appears insignificant in terms of our modern inflated dollars, is seen in its true light when it is realized that the *total* federal spending for internal improvements from the birth of our nation through 1828 amounted to $3,585,000.[18] Private giving through the churches and voluntary societies dwarfed government spending for what is now termed "health and human services."

Nineteenth-century American evangelicals saw no contradiction between evangelism and social concern. The truly converted person would demonstrate his or her faith in concern for the needy neighbor. Evangelist Edward Norris Kirk, preaching in Boston in 1842, declared that when ". . . men love their neighbors as themselves, the causes of poverty will be sought out, and the remedy applied as far as possible."[19] Kirk's outlook was not unusual among nineteenth-century evangelists. Historian Timothy Smith of Johns Hopkins University has concluded that, "far from disdaining earthly affairs, the evangelists played a key role in the widespread attack upon slavery, poverty, and greed."[20]

Phoebe Palmer, the pioneering Methodist laywoman and founder of the Five Points Mission, a settlement house for the poor in New York City, was one of many who were active in evangelical efforts to minister to the urban poor. Evangelicals were involved in seasonal and disaster relief, holiday meals and gifts, fresh air programs for children, urban medical dispensaries and clinics, the Y.M.C.A. and Y.W.C.A., rescue homes for women, employment bureaus, volunteer prison work, temperance reform, orphanages, and efforts to abolish slavery.

William Booth's Salvation Army was one of the most effective evangelical ministries to the urban poor. In a journal notation of 1868, Booth noted that "many thousands of the starving poor have been relieved." In the previous two years Booth had sponsored temperance meetings, evening classes for "reading, writing, and arithmetic," reading rooms, soup kitchens, rescue operations for "fallen girls," and unemployment services, and had helped poor people desiring to emigrate. An article in the *Cleveland Plain Dealer* admitted that "no organization of public or private charity" equaled the Army's ability to reach the very poor.[21]

The breadth and depth of evangelical social concern in the nineteenth century was such that even the secular press could not deny its impact. The *New York Observer* remarked in 1855, "Infidelity makes a great outcry about its philanthropy, but religion does the work."[22] Most of the *Observer's* readers would have concurred in that judgment: the fruits of evangelical religion were too obvious to deny.

There are now gratifying signs that evangelicals are rediscovering their historic commitment to social ministries. During the 1940s evangelical leaders such as Carl F. Henry, Harold John Ockenga, and E. J. Carnell argued that the dichotomy between evangelism and social concern was a false one, and they challenged evangelicals to demonstrate the fruits of faith in the social arena.

Today, evangelical relief organizations such as World Vision are respected around the world for their efforts in famine relief, medical work, education, and assistance in economic development. John Perkins's "Voice of Calvary" ministry in Mendenhall, Mississippi, is considered by many to be one of the most effective recent efforts in community development and self-help for the poor. The Christian Action Council, founded by evangelical theologian Harold O. J. Brown, is actively engaged in fighting abortion and in providing pro-life counseling services for women with problem pregnancies.

Ex-Watergate offender Charles Colson now visits an average of 50 state and federal prisons a year. His "Prison Fellowship" was founded in 1976 with a staff of six, solely from the royalties of his best-selling autobiography, *Born Again*. That ministry now has some 100 full-time staff in 35 states and a budget of nearly $3 million.[23] Colson ministers to the spiritual and emotional needs of the prisoners and challenges evangelicals to become involved in the work of prison reform. "Some 31 million Americans say they are evangelicals," notes Colson, "but it's a phony religious resurgence. We aren't making a difference in the lives of the people around us."

Even leaders from old-line fundamentalist traditions are beginning to recover the biblical balance of word and deed ministries. Jerry Falwell has visited refugee camps in Thailand, working with a relief organization. "If we are going to reach the hurting, starving people of the world," Falwell remarked, "we've got to earn the right to be heard."[24] Falwell's comments represent a healthy movement beyond the old polarizations that characterized conservative theology and church life earlier in this century.

The Social Security Dilemma

The well-known financial problems of the Social Security system today highlight both the limitations of government social welfare programs and the need for greater private initiatives. In 1937 workers paid 1 percent of the first $3,000 of their earnings into the fund. In 1981, the tax was 6.65 percent on the first $29,700, the result of a *1300 percent* increase in the past 20 years, with further hikes scheduled through 1990. Already for one half of all American families, Social Security taxes are higher than federal income taxes.[25] Economist Michael Boskin of Stanford has commented that unless some changes in the Social Security tax structures are made, we face the "greatest tax revolt and warfare in the history of the U.S."[26]

The basic problem faced by the system is that for some time the number of people collecting benefits has been increasing faster than the number of workers paying taxes. In 1950, the ratio of workers to beneficiaries was 17 to 1. By 1970, the ratio had fallen to 3 to 1. By the turn of the century, the ratio will be approaching 2 to 1.[27] Such a ratio would mean crushing tax burdens for younger workers.

If the Social Security system is to avoid bankruptcy without resorting to confiscatory rates of taxation, it seems clear that families and other private groups will need to assume greater financial responsibility for the care of the elderly. According to the Bible, this is precisely where the responsibility lies: with the family and the church, not with the state. Children are commanded to honor their parents (Exod. 20:12; Eph. 6:2,3), and this includes caring for them in their old age. The Christian who fails to provide for his own family is worse than an unbeliever (I Tim. 5:8). Jesus condemned the Pharisees who evaded their obligations to their parents in the name of religious devotion (Matt. 15:4-9).

The present Social Security system weakens the bonds of the family. Children now no longer provide for their own parents out of love or duty; they are compelled to provide for someone else's parents by force of law. The present system is now both financially precarious and morally questionable. Evangelical Christians have excellent biblical reasons to be among those who are advocating a return to greater reliance on family responsibility and initiatives from the private sector. Circumstances will require some painful adjustments in the Social Security system, but such adjustments should, in the long run, lead to interpersonal and even financial benefits for those who assume their scriptural responsibilities.

Will Evangelicals Respond to the Challenge?

It is easy, of course, to criticize the failures of government welfare programs and the high taxes they have produced. It is not so easy to propose positive alternatives and to assume a heavier load of personal responsibility. What is in view here is not a sudden cessation of all existing welfare programs and an immediate shift to complete reliance on the private sector. Such a shift is not in the realm of practical possibilities. A more realistic approach would be a *gradual* phasing-out of government welfare programs and a gradual assumption of these functions by families, churches, and other private agencies. With a significant measure of tax relief and adequate levels of economic growth, such a shift would be possible—even with respect to the Social Security system.

If a shift from reliance on the public to the private sector is to occur, evangelicals will need to play a significant role in providing the moral and spiritual leadership required. Only a society experiencing moral and spiritual renewal will demonstrate the sense of personal responsibility and commitment needed to provide quality care for a broad range of human needs. Unless a society finds its basic security in God, it will inevitably turn to human government to supply that need—but at the high cost of personal freedom.

The evangelical values of faith in God, commitment to work and personal responsibility, and the solidarity of the family are essential components in any lasting solution to our nation's human problems. Finding solutions to these problems in the stressful closing decades of the twentieth century will not be easy. But if evangelicals respond to these challenges in the light of biblical principles, we should find ourselves rewarded with lighter tax burdens, stronger family life, greater sensitivity to the needs of the poor, and greater credibility in our evangelistic witness.

7

Does the Bible Favor Capitalism or Socialism?

Does the Bible favor either capitalism or socialism as an economic system? The question elicits strong feelings from clergy members and the intellectual community. All too often capitalism is condemned in tones of righteous indignation as a morally corrupt enterprise.

According to Bishop Dale White of the United Methodist Church, "All of us, really, are hostages . . . to a vast political economic system of cruelty structures which are preordaining that the rich get richer and the poor get poorer. . . . These systems are . . . so powerful, so destructive . . . that perhaps the word which Khomeini used for them, the word 'Satanic,' is the only word which is aptly descriptive."[1] The "vast political economic system" is, of course, America, and the "cruelty structures" are American corporations. Bishop White does not speak for the entire Methodist Church, of course, but his comments do express a distressing tendency among the clergy to upbraid our nation's economic system.

During the Great Depression, in *Christian Message for the World Today*, a book, co-authored by a number of prominent churchmen, the "Christian message" was that the ". . . whole future of Christian societies depends on whether Christianity, or rather Christians, decisively leave off supporting capitalism and social injustice."[2] In the minds of these churchmen, "capitalism" and "social injustice" were virtually synonymous. Fifty years after the Great Depression, this mentality still finds expression in many denominational publications, seminaries, workshops, and conferences.

Norman Podhoretz, editor of the journal *Commentary*, has observed that most intellectuals have tended to look upon capitalism as an evil: "a system unsound in itself and the cause of moral and spiritual depredations throughout society as a whole."[3] Similar observations have been made by Paul Johnson, a British historian who himself formerly espoused the socialist cause. In many colleges and universities, Johnson notes, the free market system is presented as "destructive of human happiness, corrupt, immoral, wasteful, inefficient, and above all, doomed." On the other hand, some form of socialism is generally presented as"the only way out compatible with the dignity of the human spirit and the future of our race."[4] It is highly ironic that the sons and daughters of successful businessmen often enroll at prestigious colleges and universities where professors systematically attack the economic system that is paying the tuition. Business all too often fails to get good press in the classroom.

The same anti-capitalistic bias common among the clergy and the academic community is also widespread in the mass media. In one scene from the popular television series, *Dallas,* a character says to Bobby Ewing, J.R.'s younger brother, "If you try to run a business on honesty and friendship, you won't be in business long."[5] Comments like that help to perpetuate the stereotype of the successful businessman as an unscrupulous and morally corrupt individual.

Some Preliminary Questions

Is it virtually impossible to be successful in business without compromising one's Christian principles? Should Christians favor some form of socialism as a morally superior system? This chapter will answer both questions with a definite "no." Biblical principles, properly understood, favor a capitalistic or free market system.

But someone might ask, Is it even fair to expect clear answers from the Bible on matters of *economic* philosophy? and, What exactly do we mean by "socialism" and "capitalism"?

In answer to the first question, certainly the Bible's central concern is salvation and not economics. The Bible is not a textbook or technical treatise on economics, just as it is not a textbook on science, philosophy, or psychology. Nevertheless, the Bible is true and authoritative on every matter of which it speaks, whether spiritual or secular. The Word of God is a lamp unto our feet (Ps. 119:105) both for time and eternity. The principles of godliness found in Scripture hold promise for the *present life* as well as the life to come (I Tim. 4:8). While the Bible is not concerned with some of the more technical aspects of economics, it teaches basic truths concerning human nature, the character of justice, and the proper life of man in society. In other words, the Bible gives the believer a *presuppositional base* for testing the various claims and assumptions of competing systems.

In spite of claims made by some economists that their discipline is strictly "scientific" and "objective," economics, like all other human enterprises, makes assumptions about human nature and the shape of the good society. These assumptions need to be exposed and critically examined in the light of Scripture. It is the biblical teaching concerning *human nature* that tips the balance in favor of the free market system.

As for the terms "capitalism" and "socialism," some nontechnical definitions will suffice for our purposes. "Capitalism" is here used as a synonym for the "free market" or "free enterprise" system. The term "capitalism" was coined by the Marxist opponents of the free market economy and still carries pejorative overtones in the minds of many, but its use is too deeply imbedded in our language to abandon it entirely. The capitalistic or free market system is one in which the production, pricing, and distribution of goods and services is controlled predominantly by the private sector. In such a system, economic power is decentralized, and economic decisions are made by many buyers and sellers. In the classical free market model the role of government is a limited one, concerned mainly with police actions designed to protect the market participants from coercion and fraud.

"Socialism" may be defined as an economic system in which the production, pricing, and distribution of goods and services are controlled predominantly by the state. Such a system implies a greater concentration of economic power than under the free market, and a greater involvement of government in economic affairs. In a socialistic system the central government not only acts as a policeman, but, more importantly, controls the use of land, labor, and capital. This concentration of state power is usually justified in terms of an ideal of "social justice" or what is thought to be a more equitable distribution of society's goods and services.

In actual practice modern states tend to represent a blend of free market and socialistic elements. Hence the need for the term "predominantly" in the above definitions. Nevertheless, in the cases of, say, the United States and the Soviet Union, the predominance in one direction or another is clear enough to justify the common use of the terms "capitalism" and "socialism" to describe the respective economic systems.

The Case for Socialism

"From each according to his ability, to each according to his need." There is no question that these often-quoted words of Karl Marx have an idealistic appeal. In an ideal world, everyone would work to the best of his ability for the common good, and be satisfied with a reward commensurate to his needs.

The sentiments expressed by Marx reflect certain themes of the Bible, and not a few religious leaders have come to the conclusion that biblical principles favor socialism. One such religious leader is Eugene Bianchi, a professor of religion at Emory University. The arguments presented by Professor Bianchi in an article entitled "Capitalism and Christianity Revisited," which appeared in the magazine *Christian Century*, are worth examining.[6]

(1) The first criticism Bianchi brings is that capitalism fosters an intense individualism that is contrary to the biblical emphasis on

community. If capitalism did not ". . . create the Hobbsian war of all against all, it certainly cultivates the seeds of such enmity," he claims. "The self is supreme over against others."[7] In a socialistic system, on the other hand, such biblical values as community and cooperation presumably have a better chance of flourishing.

Bianchi is right in pointing to biblical values such as community and cooperation, but there are at least three weaknesses in this first criticism. It is true that the New Testament points to the new community of the body of Christ (Rom. 12; I Cor. 12) as the ideal context for fulfilling our human needs. The Bible clearly stresses the need for cooperation; we are to bear one another's burdens and so fulfill the law of Christ (Gal. 6:2). The problem with the socialist approach, however, is that it would *force* people to cooperate and *force* people to join the new Marxist community. In the New Testament, true community and cooperation are produced not by governmental coercion, but by the grace of God and the work of the Holy Spirit. The spiritual changes in human nature produced by God lead to a willing desire of the individual involved to worship and work with like-minded people. The Marxist program seeks to impose its brand of community and cooperation on people whose nature has not been changed, and history shows that over sixty years of government coercion have not succeeded in producing the "New Soviet Man."

In the American tradition, on the other hand, the individual is free to associate on a *voluntary* basis with those whose values and goals he shares. True community is formed only with the inward consent of the people involved. The rise of the independent labor union Solidarity in Poland is a striking testimony to the failure of the Soviet program of compulsory "cooperation." The Soviet versions of compulsory "community" violate the basic God-given right of freedom of association.

In the second place, Bianchi's distorted picture of capitalism as a Hobbsian "war of all against all" overlooks the elements of cooperation and interdependence that are essential to the proper functioning of the system. It is a part of the genius of the free market system that the *division of labor*, which promotes specialization of function and mutual interdependence, benefits all who are involved. If Italian cobblers have a special gift for making shoes, and American engineers have a special talent for designing computers, then it is to the advantage of both nations to specialize in those areas of excellence and engage in international trade. The free market system, at both domestic and international levels, rewards the whole society for cooperation and interdependence.

In the third place, Bianchi criticizes the free enterprise system for its "individualism," without recognizing its virtue of individual responsibility. Certainly any economic system—including socialism —can be abused by individualistic and selfish people. The strength of the free market system, however, is that it teaches individual responsibility. The Bible teaches that we will reap what we sow (Gal. 6:7), and that we all have to give an ultimate accounting of our lives before the judgment seat of Christ (II Cor. 5:10). These New Testament texts are primarily concerned with salvation, of course, but the point is that our entire lives should be lived with the idea of personal accountability in mind. A person in business is reminded daily of the fact that our actions have consequences, and this can be seen as a way of being trained and disciplined in a spiritual truth.

(2) A second criticism voiced by Professor Bianchi concerns the "materialism" associated with capitalism. "The gospel," he says, "commands us to share material goods, not to amass them."[8] Christ warns us not to lay up treasures for ourselves on earth (Matt.6:19). Does not the free enterprise system encourage people to do precisely what Christ warns against?

In the first place, it seems selective to lay the charge of "materialism" exclusively at the door of the free market system. The people of North Korea, Czechoslovakia, Poland, or the Soviet Union appear no more hesitant to enjoy refrigerators, washing machines, and automobiles than do their counterparts in the United States. In the second place, and more importantly, this criticism fails to distinguish the free market as a *mechanism* for producing, pricing, and distributing goods from the *motivation* of those who are involved in the system. There is no question that in America today materialism is a strong temptation, and that Christians, like the rich young ruler, can have their priorities in the wrong place. But it would be a great error to suppose that the free enterprise system, considered as a mechanism for producing and distributing goods and services, is inherently antithetical to the Christian ideal of serving the community through legitimate business endeavors. The lives of countless dedicated Christian men and women in business are living proof to the contrary.

(3)   A third problem Bianchi has with capitalism is that it concentrates political power in the hands of the wealthy few. "American people," he says, "are increasingly aware that our political system is a plutocracy mouthing the slogans of democracy."[9] By implication this criticism is intended to be an argument in favor of socialism, where presumably political power is not concentrated in the hands of the "wealthy few."

This argument is most unimpressive. Would Professor Bianchi really have us believe that the average person in Russia or North Korea has more influence in political affairs than the average person in America? In spite of all the rhetoric of equality, Marxist systems concentrate political power in the hands of a tiny elite—the Communist party. In our American system, political influence is much more widely dispersed. Citizens are free to organize political action groups and to lobby for their cause, whether it happens to be saving whales, stopping abortion, or protesting an unpopular war. Recent elections have demonstrated the considerable impact made by such grassroots organizations. Corporations and labor unions do have political clout, but neither of these groups exercises the type of totalitarian control over society exercised by Communist parties. And how many citizens' lobbying groups are allowed within the walls of the Kremlin?

A problem voiced by many religious critics of the free enterprise system relates to the "profit motive" and the role of self-interest. Evidently these critics feel that profit and self-interest are contrary to the biblical ideal of unselfish service to one's neighbor. The presumption would seem to be that socialism is motivated by altruism, and hence is morally preferable as an economic system.

There are at least four different weaknesses in that type of argument. In the first place, it is hardly true that altruism has replaced self-interest as the prime driving force in socialist societies. A Russian factory manager desires to "get ahead" and to be rewarded with greater power and prestige as much as his American counterpart. Sixty years of Marxist rhetoric have not succeeded in changing human nature.

In the second place, that type of criticism confuses greed and legitimate self-interest. While the Bible clearly condemns greed as sinful (I Cor. 5:11), it recognizes a legitimate form of self-interest. We are to love our neighbors *as we love ourselves*. The proper concern for our own needs and the needs of our immediate family is to be the baseline from which we extend our concern for the needs of others.

Adam Smith, author of the economic classic, *Wealth of Nations*, has been criticized for pointing to the role of self-interest in the free market economy. "It is not from the benevolence of the butcher, the brewer or the baker that we expect our dinner," he observed, "but from regard to their own interest."[10] The Bible does not condemn self-interest as such, but only immoral and criminal actions, which carry it to excesss.

In the third place, this line of criticism seems to assume that self-interest and service to the neighbor are antithetical to one another. The true situation is quite the opposite. The genius of the free market system is that it coordinates my self-interest and the needs of my neighbor. I am rewarded most when I succeed in meeting the needs of my neighbor by efficiently providing the goods and services desired. As Professor Ernest van den Haag has observed, the effect of capitalism is that "one gets rich, not by robbery and oppression, as so often in pre-capitalist times, but by producing and selling what people want."[11] The market forces one to be sensitive to the needs of others. For the Christian, this "natural" dynamic is reinforced by the example of the self-giving service of Christ, who first humbled himself as a servant, and then was highly exalted (Phil. 2:7-9).

In the fourth place, there is the question of the much-despised "profit motive." The critics seem to believe that such a motive is unworthy of a Christian. This attitude reflects a faulty understanding of the nature of profit. Those influenced by Marxist ideas tend to identify profit with "exploitation": the capitalist is "ripping off" the worker. Profit, however, is the manager's or entrepreneur's proper reward for successful efforts to meet the needs of the public efficiently by making investments, taking risks, and producing goods and services. The Bible teaches that "the laborer deserves his wages" (I Tim. 5:18). If labor deserves a reward for its efforts, so does management. The concept of profit is not condemned by the New Testament, but is presupposed in passages such as Matthew 25:14-30, the parable of the talents. There the faithful servants are commended for making profitable use of the master's money.

The desire for monetary profit can of course be taken to excess, as can virtually every human desire. The biblical approach, however, is not to condemn the desire for profit out of hand, but to infuse it with the spirit of the gospel and with the Christian ideal of service to God and the neighbor. "You shall love your neighbor as yourself" (Matt. 22:34); "Whatever you do, do all to the glory of God" (I Cor. 10:31).

The Case for Capitalism

Basic biblical principles, properly understood, point to the free market as the most desirable economic system. In the first place, consider the biblical provisions concerning the rights of *private property*. The right of the individual to buy, sell, and use property is fundamental to the free market system, and the broad ownership of property in a society is necessary to provide a check against excessive concentrations of economic power in the hands of the state.

The right of private property is presupposed in the eighth commandment, "You shall not steal" (Exod. 20:15). Elsewhere in the Old Testament law, the people of Israel are commanded not to move a neighbor's landmark (Deut. 19:14; 27:17), and not to be slack in paying a worker's wages (Lev. 19:13; cf. James 5:4), which could be a form of robbery.

In the area of trade and commerce, God commands the use of just weights and measures. "A full and just weight you shall have . . .

that your days may be prolonged in the land which the Lord your God gives you" (Deut. 25:15). The use of dishonest weights and measures is a form of theft, and is condemned as an "abomination to the Lord your God" (25:16). Modern governments violate this commandment when they debase the currency through inflationary policies. Government-sponsored inflation surreptitiously transfers wealth from one sector of society to another, and robs pensioners, annuitants, savers, stockholders, and creditors of the fruits of their investments.

The provisions for the year of Jubilee (Lev. 25), which we considered in some detail in a previous chapter, presuppose the legitimacy of private property. The intent of the Jubilee legislation was to preserve the broad ownership of property in Israel. When the prophet Micah looked forward to the blessings of the messianic age, he envisioned not vast collective farms operated by the state, but a society with "every man under *his* vine and under *his* fig tree" (Mic. 4:4).

The New Testament likewise considers private property to be legitimate. Even in the midst of the "communal sharing" of the early Jerusalem church, Peter can say to Ananias in regard to his property, ". . . after it was sold, was it not at *your* disposal?" (Acts 5:4). Passages such as I Timothy 6:17-19 presuppose differences of wealth and income within the church; any redistribution of income is to be done on a voluntary basis, as a free and cheerful response to the grace of God.

Socialistic schemes of coercive income redistribution, done in the name of compassion for the poor, violate biblical commands requiring impartial treatment for both rich and poor. "You shall not be partial to a poor man in his suit" (Exod. 23:3).

Someone might argue, in reply, that God's lordship over the entire creation relativizes or even supersedes human property rights. Is it not true that the ". . . earth is the Lord's, and the fulness thereof, the world and those who dwell therein" (Ps. 24:1)? Granted that all property ultimately belongs to God; the fallacy of redistributionist schemes, however, is to assume that a certain individual or government has the right to sit on God's throne and exercise those rights of divine ownership. God has delegated rights of ownership to human beings, and these rights are to be respected in the context of the normal affairs of society. Even Abraham, whose descendants were promised the land of Canaan by God, respected the property rights of Ephron the Hittite (Gen. 23), and paid him the full price of the burying ground for Sarah.

The institution of private property not only has the virtue of providing a check against the power of the state, but also provides a training ground for personal responsibility. The believer's orientation is toward eternity, but he or she grows in personal maturity by exercising proper stewardship in time. The principle that "he who is faithful in a very little is faithful also in much" (Luke 16:10) applies here. Material possessions are not an end in themselves, but they are a test and a training ground for cultivating faithfulness to the Master. Joseph's able stewardship of Potiphar's and Pharaoh's property (Gen. 39–41) became a source of great blessing to the children of Israel. God, who created men and women in his own image to exercise dominion over the creation (Gen. 1:26-28), intends for the believer to exercise that dominion under his or her own roof. Ability to lead in the church presupposes proven ability to manage well the affairs of one's own household (I Tim. 3:4, 12). The free enterprise system, by encouraging the broad ownership of private property, provides a superior way of developing the sense of personal responsibility, rather than mere fear of punishment by the state.

In the second place, given the biblical teachings concerning *human nature*, the free market clearly emerges as the superior economic system. The Bible clearly teaches that all men are limited in knowledge, and that all men are sinners and are born with a sinful nature. Both of these biblical teachings have profound implications for the way we evaluate economic systems.

The Bible unambiguously asserts that while God is omniscient, man most certainly is not. Not only is our knowledge of divine things limited (Deut. 29:29; Rom. 11:33); even our knowledge of temporal affairs is partial. We do not know what the next day will bring (James 4:14). One of the fatal weaknesses of socialist economic theory is that it supposes that a government planner or central committee can accurately forecast and determine the prices, supplies, and consumer demands for tens of thousands of items in a complex industrial society. Such an assumption attributes virtually godlike omniscience to the government planners.

François de Combret, a top French presidential economic adviser, once admitted, "A bureaucrat like myself [sitting in an office all day] does not know enough to make all economic decisions. Those who know what to do are the ones who have skills, the ones willing to take the risks."[12]

As economic writer George Taber has observed, "The best planning is still provided by private businessmen and women making decisions on the basis of the information they receive from consumers in the marketplace."[13]

The limited knowledge of government planners inevitably leads to inefficiencies and misallocations of resources in socialist economies. The great free market economist Ludwig von Mises put it this way: "A completely socialist society would not know how to distribute its labor, capital, land and other factors of production to the best advantage. It would not know which commodities or services it was producing at a social profit and which at a social loss."[14] The chronic shortages that plague socialist economies confirm the truth of von Mises' analysis. The Soviet Union can experience an oversupply of tractors in one year, and a shortage of corn the next.

The book of Proverbs tells us that "in an abundance of counselors there is safety" (11:14), i.e., "many heads are better than one." The merit of the free market system is that it distributes the decision-making process over a vast number of buyers and sellers, rather than concentrating such decisions in the hands of a small government elite. The free market approach casts a much wider net in the gathering of economic information, and has the further merit of leaving the decision-making power in the hands of those who must bear the responsibility for those decisions. If a businessman makes a bad decision, his profits will suffer; if a tenured government bureaucrat makes an economic miscalculation, the taxpayers are always there to absorb the costs.

One of the most basic biblical teachings about man is that human nature is sinful. It is not only that all actually commit sin (Rom. 3:23), but that we all enter this world with a sinful nature (Eph. 2:3). The importance of this teaching for our evaluation of economic systems cannot be overestimated.

One of the consequences of man's sinful nature is the tendency to abuse power. Biblical history gives many examples of the dangers of concentrated power. We have already noted Samuel's warnings to the people of Israel concerning the dangers of kingship (I Sam. 8). Those warnings of tyranny were amply confirmed in the life of Israel. One pointed example is found in I Kings 21, the account of Ahab's judicial murder of Naboth and subsequent seizure of his vineyard. Revelation 13 paints a vivid picture of the beast's persecuting the church—a symbolic portrayal of the concentrated political and economic power of a corrupt Roman Empire.

The Founding Fathers were deeply suspicious of concentrated political power and purposely enshrined a separation of powers doctrine into the U.S. Constitution. The concept of checks and balances should also be applied to a society's ordering of the relation between political and economic power. If one accepts the biblical analysis of human nature, and its warnings about the corrupting influence of concentrated power, the fatal flaw of all socialist systems becomes apparent: they concentrate both political and economic power in the hands of the state.

The contemporary writer William Barrett asks, "How could we ever have believed that you could deprive human beings of the fundamental right to initiate and engage in their own economic activity without putting every other human right in jeopardy? Everything we observe about the behavior of human beings in groups . . . should tell us that you cannot unite political and economic power in one center without opening the door to tyranny."[15] By reserving the rights of economic decision making to the private sector, the free market system provides a bulwark against the encroachments of government tyranny.

That point brings us to a third feature in which the free market manifests its superiority: the preservation and extension of human freedom. Man was created by God to be free, to exercise dominion over the earth (Gen. 1:28). It is only because of sin that man finds himself the victim of domination and tyranny. One of the fruits of the gospel is that it brings freedom to man, by abolishing slavery to sin, by restoring his dignity as an image bearer of God, and by freeing his conscience from the tyranny of merely human traditions and ideologies. "For freedom Christ has set us free; stand fast therefore and do not submit again to a yoke of slavery" (Gal. 5:1).

The free market system promotes human freedom by enhancing the rights of the individual and checking the power of the state. It is not merely coincidental that no Communist or totally socialist economy has remained a democracy for long, and that every democracy practices some version of capitalism. George Taber is certainly correct in his conclusion that in the long run, "political freedom is impossible without economic freedom."[16]

Our conclusion, then, is that the biblical teachings concerning property and the nature of man clearly point to the free market as the superior economic system. In the following chapter we will see how this conclusion is supported by the facts of human history.

8
The Lessons of History

"Leningrad can be overstocked with cross-country skis . . . and yet go several months without soap for washing dishes. I knew a Moscow family that spent a frantic month hunting for a child's potty while radios were a glut on the market."[1] These observations by Hedrick Smith, former Moscow Bureau Chief for the *New York Times*, highlight the persistent problems of a planned socialist economy.

In this chapter we will examine the respective track records of the free market and socialistic economic systems. Marx believed that history would demonstrate the inherent superiority of socialism. He predicted that capitalism would lead to progressive impoverishment of workers, and that the system itself would be destroyed by a succession of boom-and-bust cycles of increasing intensity.

Leon Trotsky, one of the key figures in the earlier phases of the Russian Revolution, had even more grandiose hopes for socialism. He believed that in a socialist society man would become "incomparably stronger, wiser, finer. His body more harmonious, his movements more rhythmical, his voice more musical. . . . the human average will rise to the level of an Aristotle, a Goethe, a

Marx. Above these other heights new peaks will arise."

History has not been kind to the utopian hopes of Marx and Trotsky. The "New Socialist Man" is yet to appear, and, as we shall see, the historical record shows that capitalism has been far more effective than socialism in improving the lot of the common man.

We will also examine some popular but mistaken notions about the track record of the free market system. Did not the "robber barons" of the nineteenth century demonstrate that industrial capitalism is a predatory and oppressive system? Did not the Great Depression demonstrate once and for all the inherent instability of the free market? In this chapter we will attempt to show that the common perception on both those questions is mistaken and only serves to obscure the real merits of the free market approach.

The Longer View

Without an adequate knowledge of the past it is easy to lose sight of the fact that the material abundance produced by industrial capitalism is a very recent phenomenon. We noted in an earlier chapter that poverty has been the usual lot of mankind for most of recorded history. The concept of a steadily growing economy was virtually unknown in ancient times. Growth rates through most of human history have been very low, zero, or negative. Pre-industrial societies were caught in a Malthusian trap of slow growth, increasing population, outstripping of food supplies, and demographic disaster.

As the British historian Paul Johnson has pointed out, prior to the eighteenth century, "it was rare for even the most advanced economies, those of England and Holland, to achieve one percent growth in any year."[2] Beginning in the 1780s, England achieved an unprecedented annual growth rate of two percent. By the end of the decade a rate of four percent had been attained—a rate that was to be sustained for the next 50 years.

During the nineteenth century, Britain increased the size of its workforce by 400 percent. Real wages doubled during the period from 1800 to 1850, and doubled again from 1850 to 1900. "This meant," notes Johnson, "there was a 1600% increase in the production and consumption of wagegoods during the century. Nothing like this had happened anywhere before in the whole of history."[3] After 1850, even higher rates of growth were being attained in Belgium, France, Austria-Hungary, Germany, and the United States. Marx's prediction that industrial capitalism would progressively impoverish the workers was falsified by the facts of history.

What produced this great "lift off" in the Western nations? The experience of England, the pioneer in the new industrial revolution, is very instructive. The sources of the dramatic progress were both technological and intellectual. Harnessing the new energy of coal and steam lifted English society to a new plateau of productivity far higher than the old economy based on the muscle of horse and man. The new ideas of Adam Smith exploded the old mercantilist notions, which measured the nation's wealth by stocks of silver and gold amassed through plunder and the cumbersome operations of a centrally controlled economy. Adam Smith's *Wealth of Nations* portrayed a vision of a society in which the initiative, energy, and imagination of countless enterprising individuals would produce a more abundant society for all. The Protestant Reformation, and later the Wesleyan revival, reinforced the biblical values of work, thrift, and personal responsibility, and thus helped create a moral climate that contributed to economic progress.

"In short," writes Paul Johnson, reviewing the trend of events, "after nearly five recorded millennia of floundering about, in relative or absolute poverty, humanity suddenly in the 1780's began to hit on the right formula: industrial capitalism."[4] And the progress was indeed dramatic. During the 1780s, 80 percent of the people of France were spending 90 percent of their income on bread, merely to stay alive. Today France has more automobiles per capita than even Germany, and more second homes than any other European country. It is important to keep facts such as these in mind as we examine particular issues relating to the nineteenth-century experience.

"Robber Barons" and "Dark, Satanic Mills"

Despite the impressive historical evidence for dramatic economic progress in Western society during the last several centuries, there is the widespread belief in the popular mind that capitalism produced enormous degradation, impoverishment, and oppression for the common man. That view can be found in novels, textbooks, newspapers, and television and radio productions today. How did it arise? Curiously enough, it was spread not only by Karl Marx and his followers, but also by countless nineteenth-century social reformers, educators, writers, and clergymen who had no particular sympathy for the doctrines of Marx. One can recall the lurid descriptions of the factory system in the novels of Charles Dickens, and the English poet William Blake's characterization of these factories as "dark, satanic mills."

The English industrial revolution had not only improved the living conditions of the masses, but also produced a fundamental alteration in society's perception of poverty. Since poverty no longer appeared to be the inevitable lot of mankind, instances of it seemed all the more to call for vigorous reform. Industrial capitalism produced a "revolution of rising expectations," and its very success provoked an outpouring of criticism. A social conscience quickened by the evangelical revivals of the nineteenth century was made more sensitive to such criticisms.

But were the English factories really "dark, satanic mills"? There is no question that conditions in many of the factories were far from ideal, but careful historical research has exploded the myth that the system led to the progressive impoverishment of workers. Exactly the opposite was the case. Economic historians W. S. Hutt and T. S. Ashton have demonstrated that while there were areas of unevenness, the general trend for English workers in the nineteenth century was one of improving standards of living. Real wages were increasing; the price of textiles fell, increasing the availability of clothing; after 1820, the price of consumer items such as tea, coffee, and sugar fell substantially. Ashton concludes that "the number of those who were able to share in the benefits of economic progress was larger than the number of those who were shut out from those benefits."⁵ Countless thousands of English men and women *voluntarily* left the farms in order to work in the factories, believing that the new system offered greater opportunities for economic betterment. And more often than not, those hopes were realized.

In 1837 or 1838, Thomas Holmes, age 87, gave to a member of the Liverpool Statistical Society his recollections of the changes in English society during his lifetime. "There has been a very great increase in the consumption of meat, wheaten bread, poultry, tea and sugar," he said. "The poorest are not so well fed. But they are better clothed, lodged and provided with furniture, better taken care of in sickness and misfortune. So they are gainers. This, I think, is a plain statement of the whole case."⁶

It is a commonly held belief that nineteenth-century America was the age of the robber barons. John D. Rockefeller, Cornelius Vanderbilt, Leland Stanford, and other predatory capitalists were milking the country dry with their rapacious, dog-eat-dog form of economic warfare. Such is the picture presented in Matthew Josephson's influential 1934 book, *The Robber Barons*. According to Josephson, the capitalistic system was the problem, and government intervention was the solution. In spite of Josephson's claims, however, a closer examination of the record discloses that the real culprit was not the *free market* system as such, but *government intervention* on behalf of privileged business interests.

A good case in point is provided by the "Credit Mobilier" scandal of the 1860s. The Credit Mobilier was a "construction" company directed by those who had controlling interests in the Union Pacific Railroad. Through their political influence Congress passed the Pacific Railroad bill in 1862, granting the Union Pacific Railroad 12,000,000 acres of land and $27 million in six percent, thirty-year government bonds as a first mortgage, and 9,000,000 acres of land and $24 million in government bonds to the Central Pacific Railroad. The project was to establish rail connections between Omaha, Nebraska, and the Great Salt Lake. Financial interests in the Union Pacific Railroad used the Credit Mobilier to subcontract the construction work to themselves, and when construction costs mysteriously skyrocketed, the profits reaped by the Credit Mobilier were enormous. When the swindle became known, the public outcry against *"laissez-faire* capitalism" was immediate. But as Susan L. Brown and other authors in *The Incredible Bread Machine* have pointed out, capitalism was being blamed unfairly. The promoters of the Credit Mobilier raised their capital not by private investment but by government subsidy—by "subsidies, franchises, land grants and associated government involvements which are not characteristic of laissez faire capitalism."[7] The Credit Mobilier was not a true example of the free market, but of its perversion through the use of government power for the sake of special privilege. In this case "big business" was reaping profits not through fair competition in the open market, but through manipulating the political system for its own ends.

John D. Rockefeller's Standard Oil Company is frequently cited as the prime example of the evils of monopoly capitalism in the nineteenth century. According to the authors of one popular college text, "Rockefeller was a ruthless operator who did not hesitate to crush his competitors by harsh and unfair methods."

As economist Lawrence W. Reed has pointed out, such charges present a distorted picture of the reasons for Rockefeller's financial success. According to Reed, Rockefeller's profits stemmed not from a *coercive* monopoly produced by government grants of exclusive privilege, but from an *efficiency* monopoly—a concentration of the market produced by a company's excellence in satisfying its customers. Even Ida Tarbell, one of Rockefeller's most persistent critics, admired the efficiency of his operations. Describing one of Standard Oil's refineries, Tarbell admitted that it was "a marvelous example of economy, not only in materials, but in time and in footsteps." Economic historian D. T. Armentano has pointed out that between 1870 and 1885 Standard Oil reduced its refining costs for kerosene from 3 cents per gallon to less than .5 cents per gallon. "Clearly," notes Armentano, "the firm was relatively efficient, and its efficiency was being translated to the consumer in the form of lower prices for a much improved product, and to the firm in the form of additional profits."[8]

Did Standard Oil ruthlessly drive out its competitors through predatory price cutting? Reed cites the conclusion of historian Gabriel Kolko: "Standard attained its control of the refinery business primarily by mergers, not price wars, and most refinery owners were anxious to sell out to it. Some of these refinery owners later reopened new plants after selling to Standard."

Unlike the Credit Mobilier, John D. Rockefeller's profits did not derive from special subsidies and privileges granted by the government. While Rockefeller certainly wanted to make money, a fair reading of the facts discloses that he succeeded in doing so by the socially beneficial mechanism of the free market—by efficiently producing a quality product that the public really wanted to buy.

The Great Depression

More than any other event in the twentieth century, the Great Depression succeeded in convincing a generation of Americans that the free market system, left to itself, simply could not work. The social impact of this event was enormous. Some 12 million Americans were unemployed; some 5,000 banks and 86,000 businesses failed; in 1932 alone, 273,000 families were evicted from their homes. Despair and a sense of helplessness gripped the country. People knocked on doors for handouts, and some even fought for leftovers in the alleys behind restaurants. Journalist Saul Pett expressed the common view of the matter in his observation that the Depression was "the watershed, the great turn in history in which laissez-faire died and the basic philosophy of American government was profoundly altered."[9] Only the resources of the federal government, so it seemed, could rescue the nation from the wreckage of the free enterprise system.

But was that really the case? Recent economic research has questioned this common view, presenting facts that show that government intervention was more a cause than a cure of the nation's economic crisis. A good measure of the blame must be laid at the feet of the Federal Reserve System, which presided over a reckless expansion of credit during the years 1924 to 1929. Professor Hans

Sennholz, a noted conservative economist, has argued that this credit expansion made the crash of 1929 inevitable. "Inflation and credit expansion always precipitate business maladjustments and malinvestments that must later be liquidated," he writes.[10] Even after the monetary collapse began, the Federal Reserve did not take responsible countermeasures. According to Milton Friedman, the evidence is now conclusive that "the System not only had a legislative mandate to prevent the monetary collapse, but could have done so if it had wisely used the powers that had been granted to it in the Federal Reserve Act."[11]

The Smoot-Hawley Tariff Act of 1930 represented another misguided government intervention, which only served to deepen the economic crisis. By raising U.S. tariffs to record levels, this action virtually closed our borders to foreign goods, provoked retaliatory tariffs on American products, and contributed to unemployment at home and abroad. Sennholz points out that U.S. exports dropped dramatically from $5.5 billion in 1929 to $1.7 billion in 1932.

The federal government compounded the nation's economic woes with the Revenue Act of 1932, doubling the federal income tax burden. This sharpest tax increase in the nation's history, designed to "soak the rich," contributed greatly to the downward spiral. "This blow alone," notes Sennholz, "would bring any economy to its knees, and shatters the silly contention that the Great Depression was a consequence of economic freedom."

Franklin D. Roosevelt's "New Deal" received the lion's share of credit for lifting the country out of the Depression, but it was really due to circumstances beyond government's control—the beginning of the Second World War—that the nation's unemployment problems were solved. The real lesson of 1929 is not that the free market system can't work, but that misguided government interventions in the market can produce far more damage than they propose to cure.

The Recent Past

Karl Marx expected industrial capitalism increasingly to impoverish workers, and finally to destroy itself in a series of boom-and-bust cycles. History has demonstrated that Marx was wrong on both counts. As George Taber has noted, "Rather than pushing workers deeper into poverty . . . capitalism has lifted the vast majority of laborers into the middle class."[12] Workers in free market economies have far more influence on management's decisions than their counterparts in Marxist societies.

Capitalism has weathered some severe fluctuations in the business cycle—the worst being the great Depression—but the predictions of its demise have turned out to be premature. Even its critics have been forced to admit its staying power as an economic system. Writes Robert Heilbroner, a left-leaning economist and persistent critic, "History has shown capitalism to be an extraordinarily resilient, persisting and tenacious system, perhaps because its driving force is dispersed among so much of its population rather than concentrated solely in a governing elite."[13]

In the Soviet Union, the inherent problems of a centrally planned economy have become increasingly evident during recent years. After dramatic productivity gains from initially low bases in the 1950s and 1960s, economic growth in Russia dropped to two percent in 1979, the lowest since the 1930s.

Lagging farm productivity has long been a weak spot in the Soviet system. In 1930 the peasants revolted against Stalin's forced collectivization and confiscation of their land and livestock. The subsequent famine was one of the worst in history, costing an estimated two to five million lives.

Problems with the collective farms have persisted down to the present day. In 1980 Soviet planners set a goal of 235 million tons of grain, but the actual harvest was only 189.2 million tons, according to official figures. Socialist Russia on many occasions has had to depend on the capitalist economies of the United States and Canada to provide bread for its own people. Late in 1981, facing another poor grain harvest, Soviet authorities mounted a public relations campaign designed to convince Russian housewives of the virtues of cooking with stale bread. "You will be rewarded by delicious, unusual dishes," an official government leaflet promised.[14]

The system of forced collective farming has not succeeded in extinguishing the spirit of free enterprise in the hearts of the Russian people. Privately farmed plots in Russia, averaging less than an acre in size, represent only three percent of Soviet farmland and yet produce an astonishing one-fourth of all Russian farm products.[15] The "New Soviet Man," when left on his own, can be as energetic and productive as his American counterpart.

The chronic inefficiency of a centrally planned economy shows itself in persistent shortages of consumer goods in the retail stores. Towels, toothpaste, axes, locks, vacuum cleaners, irons, kitchen china, cameras, or cars—the list is virtually endless. Soviet women are accustomed to spending two hours in line, seven days a week, in hopes of finding the items they want. "I have known of people who stood in line ninety minutes to buy four pineapples," writes former Moscow correspondent Hedrick Smith, "and three and a half hours to buy large heads of cabbage, only to find the cabbages were gone as they approached the front of the line."[16] Bribery of clerks is a common way of trying to obtain retail items in short supply.

The political unrest in Poland and the rise of the independent labor union Solidarity has made the West much more aware of the economic problems in that socialist society. The frustrations of the ordinary Polish citizen express the crisis of the system in a very personal way. "I do not even want to talk about food supplies," said one elderly man on a shopping trip. "There is nothing to buy, beginning with milk and ending in detergents. You have to have plenty of time or very good connections, but they do not even work anymore."[17]

Concern over a possible Russian invasion and maneuvers by Soviet troops on Poland's borders during 1981 were often over-shadowed by a preoccupation with food shortages. "Maneuvers? Yes, I'm making maneuvers—trying to get some ham for me and my daughter," commented Iadwiga Glowacka, a Warsaw technician standing in a meat shop line.[18]

A Christian minister from the United States was visiting in Gorzow, Poland, during the summer of 1981. The hostess prepared a generous Polish meal, even borrowing sausage from a neighbor. But at the table she broke down and cried, "Forty years after the war, and this is all we have." The Polish people are not starving, but staples are scarce, and meat is "all going to feed the Red Army," as one person at the table said.[19]

In our own hemisphere, the Cuban economy is a prime example of the failures of a socialist system. Prior to Castro's revolution Cuba was fourth among Latin American nations in a per capita GNP; now it is fourteenth, with one-third the rate of Puerto Rico. Rationing, inefficiency, and waste characterize the system. Milk, fruit, and vegetables are in short supply, and rice is rationed at five pounds per person per month. The Cuban economy is kept afloat by massive Soviet aid, to the tune of $3 billion a year, or $8 million a day. Castro's socialist revolution failed to deliver the equality and abundance it promised. "Cuba today is a totalitarian society in which nearly every form of dissent is severely punished," writes John W. Cooper, a researcher for the American Enterprise Institute in Washington. "Castro and his ideology not only suppress the self-determination of freedom of conscience of the Cuban people; they have also created a stagnant economy with perpetual shortages, which is completely dependent on a foreign power, the Soviet Union."[20]

In socialist states of Asia the spirit of free enterprise persists. A recent television newscast from Vietnam showed bare state-controlled food markets in Hanoi. The private street markets had plenty of food, and Vietnamese Communist leaders have admitted they need Western help for economic development. In China, nearly 5,000 veteran entrepreneurs have been given new jobs as factory managers and advisers. Hu Qiamu, director of the Chinese Academy of Social Sciences, has admitted that China has had to adopt free market principles such as "the pricing system, the rule of value, and the advantage of material incentives."[21]

Asian states such as Japan, South Korea, Taiwan, Singapore, and Hong Kong, which have given free reign to free market principles, have surged far ahead of their socialist competitors. George Taber notes that the economy of Hong Kong grew at a phenomenal 12.75 percent annual rate during four recent years, increasing real per capita income by 25 percent. During the last twenty years the economy of Singapore has increased fivefold, giving its people a standard of living second in Asia only to Japan. So many new jobs have been created by Singapore's free market economy, notes David Reed, that the residents shun menial work, "and reportedly some 100,000 'guest workers' had to be recruited from Malaysia for this purpose."[22]

The record of history, then, seems clear. In the competition between capitalism and socialism to provide both individual freedom and material abundance, capitalism wins hands down. Even its critics have admitted the free market's ability to produce and have reluctantly adopted some of its principles. The free enterprise system is consistent with biblical teachings concerning the rights and dignity of the individual, and heeds biblical warnings about the dangers of concentrating power in the hands of the state. "By limiting the state," argues theologian Michael Novak, "democratic capitalism liberates the energies of individuals and whole communities."[23] Greater abundance for all is the result.

The free market has its imperfections and failings, to be sure, but history shows that those of its competitors are far worse. George Taber is surely correct in his assessment: "For all its obvious blemishes and needed reforms, capitalism alone holds out the most creative and dynamic force that any civilization has ever discovered: the power of the free, ambitious individual."[24] When the dynamism of a society of free individuals is tempered and permeated by biblical values, the resulting system would appear to be the best one attainable by imperfect individuals this side of eternity.

9

Pollution and Depletion: Inevitable Fruits of Capitalism?

"The environmental crisis," argues ecologist Barry Commoner, "raises the fundamental question of whether the basic operational requirements [of capitalism] are compatible with ecological imperatives."[1] Earlier chapters addressed the issues of whether capitalism produced poverty and social inequality. The question now arises, Does capitalism inevitably produce pollution and resource depletion? And has Protestant theology aided and abetted the capitalistic system in an attack upon the environment? What does the Bible have to say about the Christian's environmental responsibility? These are some of the issues to be addressed in the present chapter.

The Bible and the Ecological Crisis

According to Jeremy Rifkin, author of *The Emerging Order: God in the Age of Scarcity*, a good deal of the blame for the "unrestrained pillage and exploitation of the natural world" can be placed on the shoulders of a misguided notion of "dominion" presumably long taught by Christian theology. Fortunately, says Rifkin, the concept of dominion deriving from Genesis 1:28 has "suddenly and dramat-

98

ically been reinterpreted." According to this new interpretation, "God's first instruction to the human race is to serve as a steward and protector over all of his creation."[2]

Rifkin is not the only contemporary critic to blame the Christian tradition for our environmental woes. According to environmental scientist Lynn White, Jr., by destroying the old pagan animism, "Christianity made it possible to exploit nature in a mood of indifference to the feelings of natural objects." By undermining the old animistic beliefs that gods and spirits dwelt in rocks and trees, Christianity presumably opened the floodgates of abuse upon the natural order. "We shall continue to have a worsening ecologic crisis," White goes on to say, "until we reject the Christian axiom that nature has no reason for existence save to serve man." According to White, the solution is to be found in the nature mysticism of Francis of Assissi, which presumably substitutes the idea of the "equality of all creatures, including man, for the idea of man's limitless rule of creation."[3]

Both Rifkin and White have unfortunately confused some abuses perpetrated in the name of Christianity with the teachings of the Bible itself. Rifkin mistakenly believes that the idea that man is to be a steward and protector of the earth is a new concept in Protestant theology. Rifkin was evidently unaware, for example, of John Calvin's commentaries on the creation passages in Genesis, in which he stresses the theme of stewardship and commends a "frugal" and "moderate" use of the natural order.[4] Francis Schaeffer, in *Pollution and the Death of Man*, writes that "we are to exercise our dominion over these things not as though entitled to exploit them, but as things borrowed or held in trust. . . . Man's dominion is under God's Dominion and under God's Domain."[5] Professor Henlee Barnette, in his book, *The Church and the Ecological Crisis*, observes that in Genesis 1:28, "to subdue and to have dominion over all the earth cannot mean that man has the right to destroy it for his own selfish ends."[6] And commenting on Genesis 2:15, Barnette notes that "man is placed in the garden not for mere sensual pleasure, but for responsible service."[7]

It is hardly fair for the critics to blame the Bible for the environmental abuses perpetrated by the secularized elements of a nominally Christian civilization. Modern science and technology indeed spring from biblical roots, but like so many other things beneficial in themselves, the tools of science and technology can be misused for selfish, sinful ends. By identifying the abuses with the essential biblical teaching, there is a real danger of "throwing the baby out with the bath water."

The Bible, properly understood, gives a broad basis for the Christian's environmental responsibility. As we have already noted, the mandate to exercise dominion in Genesis 1:28 means responsible stewardship of the earth, not its selfish exploitation. Man was placed in the garden (Gen. 2:15) to tend it and keep it, not to destroy it. After the flood, the covenant God makes with Noah extends to every living creature (Gen. 9:10, 12, 15, 16) and to the earth itself (v. 13), demonstrating God's concern for the world he had made. God's concern for animals is shown in Exodus 20:8-10, which includes domestic animals in the provisions for sabbath rest. The ox was not to be muzzled when it was treading out the grain (Deut. 25:4). Every seven years the land itself was to enjoy a sabbath rest (Lev. 25:4). This sabbatical provision, which spiritually typified the sabbath rest of the people of God (cf. Heb. 4:9, 10), would also have had the beneficial effect of allowing the land to renew its natural fertility. The entire natural order exists to give glory to the God who made it (cf. Ps. 19:1, the heavens are telling the glory of God). In the birds of the air and the lilies of the field the Lord Jesus sees revelations of God's care for his children (Matt. 6:26-29). The created order abounds with such signposts of God. And the time is coming, teaches the apostle Paul, when the creation itself will be liberated from its bondage to frustration and decay to enjoy the glorious liberty of the children of God (Rom. 8:20, 21). The apostle looks forward not to the annihilation but to the transformation and renewal of God's created order.

There is no need, then, to turn to Eastern religions or nature mysticism to find a religious basis for environmental concern. There are abundant theological resources for such concern in the Bible itself. As Christians we need to do a more consistent and effective job of teaching and practicing those biblical insights, so that in our environmental stewardship, as in the other areas of life, whatever we do might be done to the glory of God (I Cor. 10:31).

Profits and Pollution

"Man is poisoning his world," declares science writer Joseph Myler. "He has been labelled, with strong justification, the dirty animal." According to Myler, man has "managed to make his rivers rotten. He has transformed green pastures into deserts. He has clogged the air with chemicals which menace health and dust which is changing the climate. He is a menace to himself and other species."

Such a litany of environmental woes has become familiar to anyone living in twentieth-century America. In many cases the unspoken assumption is that industrial capitalism inevitably produces insoluble problems of pollution. While such a perspective points to matters of genuine concern for anyone living in the modern world, such constructions also have their own limitations. All too often such descriptions lack a sense of proper historical perspective, tend to exaggerate the magnitude of the problem, and frequently ignore signs of significant improvement.

Popular discussions of environmental problems tend to give the impression, for example, that pollution is a completely man-made and modern phenomenon, a creature of the industrial age. This is hardly the case. A single volcano can release as much dust into the atmosphere as several years' industrial activity.[8] An average hurricane releases the energy of 100,000 hydrogen bombs. The ten million tons of man-made pollutants released in the atmosphere must be measured against the 1,600 million tons of methane gas emitted each year by natural swamps. Forests and other forms of vegetation discharge 170 million tons of various hydrocarbons into the atmosphere each year. These latter figures, cited by historian Paul Johnson in his book *The Enemies of Society*,[9] do not mean that we should have no concern for the problems of industrial pollution. They do, however, provide a much-needed check against magnifying such problems out of all due proportion.

Examples of exaggerated claims of environmental hazards are not hard to find. Rachel Carson in her famous book, *Silent Spring*, alarmed the public with warnings about the allegedly devastating effects of chemical pesticides such as DDT. According to a special committee appointed by the National Academy of Sciences, such claims by Carson and other environmentalists were exaggerated. The special committee, appointed to advise the Environmental Protection Agency, concluded that "the chronic toxicity studies on DDT have provided no indication that the insecticide is unsafe for humans when used in accordance with commonly recognized practice."[10]

Agricultural scientist Norman E. Borlaug, winner of the 1970 Nobel Peace Prize for his work on new strains of wheat, which made the "green revolution" possible, gave the following testimony before a congressional committee in 1971: "It is a tragic error to believe that agricultural chemicals are a prime factor in the deterioration of the environment. The indiscriminate cancellation, suspension, or outright banning of such pesticides as DDT is a game of dominoes we will live to regret."[11] Similar sentiments are voiced by agriculture consultant William Boyd, who observed that "DDT has saved more lives, prevented more illness and protected more food, in the parts of the world where it is most needed, than any other chemical synthesized by man."[12] While any chemical substance can be misused, the possible dangers of a pesticide such as DDT must be measured against its real and vast benefits in alleviating human hunger and saving human lives. Environmental alarmism would endanger more lives than it seeks to protect.

After a bad oil spill in the Santa Barbara Channel, *Life* magazine reported that the channel was "a sea gone dead." Yet more careful studies by Dr. Dale Strangham found that such claims were exaggerated. There was no increase in mortality among whales or seals, and no ill effects on animal or vegetable plankton were detected. "Of 12,000 birds in the channel at the time of the spill, 3,500 to 4,000 died from all causes," according to Strangham. "Yet by May," he noted, "the bird population had risen to 85,000 because of seasonal migrations."[13]

Recent studies in oceanography have indicated that the seas have greater powers to cleanse themselves than anyone had imagined a decade ago. "There was a view ten years ago that the ocean was a very fragile thing," commented Derek Spencer, a researcher at the Woods Hole Oceanographic Institution in Massachusetts in a *Time* magazine interview. "The ocean," he said, "has some important self-cleaning processes that we didn't know about until recently."[14] The dumping of industrial wastes must still be carefully monitored, but fears of the imminent "eco-death" of the world's oceans seem to have faded.

The reporting of environmental issues has focused on the "crises," and has tended to ignore areas of genuine improvement. The result has been to leave an unbalanced picture of environmental realities in the public's mind.

In a detailed article in *Science*, Professor J. L. Simon of the University of Illinois called attention to the fact that the total acreage in the United States devoted to wildlife areas and state and national parks increased from 8 million acres in 1920 to 73 million acres in 1974. And despite fears among some environmentalists that the country's open land is rapidly being turned into parking lots and shopping centers, *all* the land used for urban areas plus roadways still amounts to less than three percent of the area of the United States. Lake Erie, pronounced environmentally dead some time ago by Barry Commoner, has improved significantly, and the fish catch is actually increasing.[15]

Substantial gains have been made in air quality. According to a report in the *Los Angeles Times*, many large industries, such as oil refineries and chemical plants, have already succeeded in controlling 90 to 95 percent of their airborne emissions.[16]

The conventional wisdom assumes that greater energy use has led to a deterioration of the human environment. While there undeniably has been some environmental damage, such an analysis is far too simplistic and overlooks the positive gains. James A. Weber has pointed out that greater energy consumption has greatly reduced the number of fatal or disabling accidents, by reducing the amount of dangerous and arduous work done by humans. He notes that the National Safety Council has reported that "between 1912 and 1977 accidental deaths per 100,000 population were reduced 41 percent from 82 to 48."[17] These figures are all the more significant when one considers the dramatic increase in the use of automobiles during that period.

The most important single indicator of overall environmental quality is life expectancy. In the United States, life expectancy has continued to rise, and at an increasing rate, as Professor Simon has pointed out. During the period 1970 to 1976, there was a gain of 2.1 years, compared with a gain of only 0.8 years during the entire decade of the 1960s.[18]

The "environment" includes not only air and water, but also sanitation, medical care, education, and working conditions. When twentieth-century conditions in America are compared with those of a century ago, the dramatic progress is apparent. The improved life expectancy figures bear witness to this improvement.

In all fairness it must be acknowledged that the environmental lobby is to be given credit for some of the progress made. At the same time, however, we have seen that a good deal of the "environmental crisis" has been overplayed by the media, and the real environmental gains overlooked. In any case, the contention that a growing free market economy inevitably destroys the environment is simply not supported by the facts.

A second major area of environmental concern involves the problem of resource depletion. Does capitalism, predicated on continuing economic growth, threaten to deplete all the world's resources?

Back in 1972, a team of Massachusetts Institute of Technology scientists, in the headline-grabbing book *Limits to Growth*, were sounding apocalyptic warnings: "Possibly within as little as 70 years, our social and economic system will collapse unless drastic changes are made very soon." The implication was that either the capitalistic system or economic growth or possibly both would have to be abandoned in order to avoid environmental and social catastrophe. The MIT scientists have since dramatically revised their predictions, but the impression lives on that our resources are in imminent danger of running out.

There are at least four major weaknesses in the "resource depletion —no growth" argument against the free market system. In the first place, history has shown that past estimates of resource reserves have been notoriously inaccurate. A 1944 survey indicated that by 1973 the United States would have exhausted its supplies of tin, nickel, lead, and manganese.[19] In fact, however, more deposits of these metals were discovered in the United States than during the previous 25 years. Progress in mining and refining technology has made possible the recovery of copper from ore that only a decade ago was worthless rock.

A 1918 estimate at the site of the Climax molybdenum mine placed reserves at six million tons of ore. "Since then," noted an article in the *Wall Street Journal*, "426 million tons have been extracted. And today there are still 433 million tons of *proven* ore reserves down there."[20]

In 1975 the U.S. Geological Survey estimated that natural gas reserves were in danger of running out shortly after the year 2000. Since then, deregulation of the industry and new computer-assisted exploration techniques have dramatically altered the picture. New discoveries of natural gas in the Rockies, the Appalachians, the Gulf Coast, and in Wyoming and Utah have led some scientists to predict that known natural gas reserves can take the United States well into the twenty-first century, and possibly even to the end of it.[21]

Events of recent years, especially the rise of the OPEC oil cartel, have focused the public's attention on our supplies of petroleum. Here again, estimates of known reserves have been wide of the mark. In 1942 estimates of world reserves of crude oil were placed at 600 billion barrels. In 1970, geologists at Mobil were estimating two trillion. In 1973, Peter Odell, reporting in the *Geographic Journal*, estimated a resource base of four trillion barrels by the year 2000.[22]

Part of the problem lies in the inadequate definition used by the U.S. Geological Survey, according to Dr. Joseph Barnea, a former director of natural resource studies at the United Nations. A *Wall Street Journal* editorial citing Dr. Barnea notes that the survey defines crude oil as "a natural mixture of hydrocarbons occurring underground in a liquid state in porous-rock reservoirs and remaining in a liquid state as it flows from a well at atmospheric pressure." According to Barnea, this definition excludes perhaps 85 percent of the crude oil that can be brought up under pressure, plus all non-liquid petroleum found in tar and sand and oil shale deposits. The result is that many published reports concerning recoverable oil overlook much of the oil actually in place. "There are plenty of hydrocarbons to last until solar power comes in," the editorial concludes, "so long as we will pay the cost of retrieving them."[23]

A second weakness in many of the more apocalyptic analyses of resource depletion is that they tend to overlook the normal workings of the law of supply and demand. Rising prices for a commodity tend to keep demand in check. And, note William J. Baumol and Wallace Oates of Princeton, higher prices also provide increased incentives to recover and recycle used resources.[24]

Since the quadrupling of oil prices by the OPEC cartel, oil consumption in the United States and other countries has been decreasing sharply. Fred Singer, a professor of environmental science, noted that throughout the world "oil is being replaced wherever possible by cheaper fuels. . . . These shifts, coupled with conservation, will cut world consumption of oil in half by the next decade."[25] Singer expects North America to become essentially self-sufficient in oil, with hardly any imports needed from overseas producers.

Predictions of imminent depletion of minerals and energy frequently overlook the significance of changing patterns of work. By the mid–1970s America's work force had experienced a remarkable transformation. More people were involved in the manipulation of information than were employed in mining, agriculture, manufacturing, and personal services combined. In fact, according to futurologist Alvin Toffler, only nine percent of the American population (20 million workers) actually manufacture goods. The other 65 million provide services and manipulate symbols.[26] This dramatic trend toward an information and service-based economy means that economic growth and wealth are no longer primarily dependent on the direct extraction of resources from the ground. The burgeoning field of microcomputers is a prime example of how new jobs and income can be generated from new ideas and human creativity without destroying the environment.

Pessimistic forecasts concerning resource availability do not take adequate account of the dramatic new gains in efficiency and productivity that are made possible through technological advances. While the earth's resources are finite, the practical question is *how* finite, and whether or not the "limits to growth" have actually been reached. History shows that human imagination and inventiveness have again and again stretched those limits beyond what society thought possible.

Today, a single communications satellite can provide the intercontinental telephone connections that in an earlier day would have required thousands of tons of copper. In real terms, a new invention has increased the supply of copper.

New technologies will be arriving during the 1990s, with great potential for dramatically altering the worlds of work and leisure. It is expected that by 1990 computers will be one hundred times faster than today's most powerful models. A single thumbnail size silicon chip will be capable of holding not 65,000 bits of data, but 1,000,000. "Computers will be about the size of a basketball and will do more than today's largest mainframes," predicted William G. Howard, Jr., of Motorola's Semiconductor Group in an interview with *Business Week*.[27]

New ceramics are being developed that will be ductile like metals, conduct electricity, and be much stronger and more durable than the products now available. These ceramics are made from metal oxides which constitute almost 90 percent of the earth's crust, thus assuring a virtually limitless supply of raw materials for the new products.

New techniques of corrosion control are being developed, which could dramatically reduce the figure of $70-90 *billion* worth of damage done each year. New technology can thus mean entirely new plateaus for the conservation of goods and resources.[28]

In the field of biotechnology, exciting new developments are in the offing. Researchers have created new varieties of bacteria that can convert industrial feedstocks into sugar and turn wood wastes into alcohol. By the 1990s these new processes could represent new multibillion dollar industries.

Significant new breakthroughs are on the horizon in the area of energy resources. Japan is already experimenting with floating platforms that generate electricity from wave power. Technology for converting garbage to fuel should become increasingly common. Within a decade cost-efficient photovoltaic cells, which convert sunlight directly into electricity, should be commercially available for home use. One firm, Arco Solar, claims that it will be selling economical home-sized arrays by the mid–1980s.[29]

Even the scientists who published the pessimistic *Limits to Growth* in 1972 are now revising their former scenarios. In their latest book, *Beyond the Age of Waste*, these scientists now state that "nuclear energy alone is capable of supplying four times the present world population with twice the current U.S. level of per capita energy consumption." Solar and geothermal will add to the energy mix, and substitutes can be found for the few raw materials that may be really scarce. *Beyond the Age of Waste* represents a remarkable turnaround from the dire predictions of 1972.

If there are indeed some legitimate grounds for a hopeful outlook on the world's energy and resource future, why does so much "bad news" abound in this area? Professor Julian Simon both raises that question and suggests some possible answers. Some groups and individuals have, in effect, vested interests in the dissemination of gloom-and-doom scenarios. "Bad news sells books, newspapers, and magazines," notes Simon; "good news is not half as interesting."[30] Is it any wonder, he asks, that there are plenty of best sellers warning about pollution, population growth, and natural-resource depletion, but few telling the facts about environmental improvement? What John Maddox has called the "doomsday syndrome" has spawned a profitable growth industry in America.

Sociologist Peter Berger has described the growth of the "New Class" in America, a class comprising many in the media, the universities, and government agencies. The New Class has a vested interest in environmental "bad news." Each new crisis helps to sell air time, create demand for new books, and justify new studies, research grants, and new rules and regulations that increase the power of bureaucrats employed in government agencies. Members of the New Class, Berger notes, tend to be hostile toward the idea of economic growth and toward the business community in general.[31]

Apart from any vested interests involved, some environmentalists may be prone to paint darker pictures than the facts really warrant out of a desire to mobilize individuals and institutions to action. In the long run, however, such "crying wolf" will lead to a serious loss of credibility for the legitimate concerns of environmental stewardship. As Philip Handler, then president of the National Academy of Sciences, once commented, "The nations of the world may yet pay a dreadful price for the public behavior of scientists who depart from . . . fact to indulge . . . in hyperbole."[32]

The Christian will certainly heed the legitimate warnings concerning possible threats to the environment and will support efforts to conserve the world's resources. At the same time, in light of the biblical covenant of dominion given in Genesis, the Christian community should seek to combine an ethic of conservation with one of creativity and innovation. As image bearers of God, men and women are endowed with creative minds that can invent new processes and devices for producing a richer life for all. "No growth" mentalities harm those who most need the fruits of new productivity, namely, the impoverished peoples of the underdeveloped nations. The biblical ethic of environmental stewardship challenges the Christian community to combine conservation and productivity, and to face the problems of the present with realism, while looking to the future with faith, courage, and hope.

10
Personal Dimensions of Christian Stewardship

"Upward mobility," George Gilder has said, "depends on work, family, and faith. . . . These are the pillars of a free economy and a prosperous society."[1] It has become increasingly clear during recent years that long-term solutions to economic problems cannot ignore the crucial contributions made by the home and family to the attitudes, habits, and values of the individuals whose aspirations and efforts are the driving forces of our economic system. The wealth or poverty of any society, and its response to changing human needs, cannot be separated from the character of its people. It is appropriate, then, that we conclude our discussion of the larger issues of wealth, poverty, and political economy by focusing on important aspects of Christian stewardship that relate specifically to our personal and family responsibilities. Biblical principles of stewardship must be practiced in our own homes and passed on to our children. As Dr. Gary North has rightly noted, "If the concept of private property is worth defending, and if personal responsibility is the moral basis of private property, then the family must be the scene of the child's introduction to the responsibilities of ownership."[2]

The Stewardship of Money

"Liberality disposes us to spend money for others' good," said Aristotle, noting how our use of money is a reflection of our character. Jesus said, "He who is faithful in little will also be faithful in much,"[3] indicating the integral relation between our stewardship of money and our faithfulness to God. In an age characterized by economic anxiety, it is especially important for the Christian to understand biblical principles of stewardship.

The Bible makes it clear that God is the ultimate and original owner of all that exists. "The earth is the Lord's, and the fulness thereof; the world, and they that dwell therein" (Ps. 24:1). This is fundamental for any proper understanding of Christian stewardship. The original right of ownership is God's, since he is the infinite Creator and preserver of all. The Christian is called to be a wise and faithful steward of the Master's possessions, knowing that an ultimate accounting will have to be given. Our money is not our own, but is to be dedicated to the Lord along with the rest of our resources as a living sacrifice (Rom. 12:1), as part of our spiritual service to God.

The Bible clearly teaches the necessity and value of regular savings and investment. Not providing for the needs of one's own family is tantamount to denying the faith (I Tim. 5:8). Honest employment is to provide for present needs (II Thess. 3:10), and careful saving is recommended to provide for the future.

According to the wisdom of Proverbs, "He that gathers in summer is a wise son, but he that sleeps in harvest causes shame" (10:5). The sluggard is admonished to learn from the ant, who gathers in summer for the winter's coming needs (6:6-8; 30:24,25). The good man, through his diligence and faithful stewardship, leaves an inheritance to his children's children (13:22).

In the New Testament, the parable of the talents (Matt. 25:14-30) teaches the obligation to invest our resources in ways that yield the maximum benefit for the Master's interests. The faithful use of present resources is rewarded with greater responsibilities and authority in the service of the kingdom: "Well done, good and faithful servant; you have been faithful over a few things; I will make you ruler over many things" (v. 25).

A good deal of our society's economic problems during recent years is a reflection of an orientation toward the present and a neglect of savings and investment for future needs. Government welfare programs and the Social Security system have weakened individual motivation to save for the future. Lowered levels of savings have reduced the amounts of capital available to business and industry for investment in new plants and equipment, and American productivity has lagged as a result. A society like our own, which becomes preoccupied with the gratification of desires in the present, will inevitably find itself becoming impoverished in the future.

The Christian, on the other hand, not only has the admonitions of Scripture concerning the wisdom of saving and investing, but has the resources of divine grace to temper present desires in the interest of a long-range good. By restricting immediate consumption, exercising wisdom and foresight, and saving for the future, the Christian, like Joseph (Gen. 41), can become a source of blessing not only to his immediate family but to the society at large as well. The biblical ethic of self-restraint, hard work, and saving for the future promoted by the Protestant Reformation was a major factor in building the capital base that made the Industrial Revolution and the prosperity of the modern West possible.

Tithing is an essential component in any program of Christian stewardship. The custom is an ancient one among the people of God, being practiced by Abraham (Gen. 14:17-20) and Jacob (Gen. 28:22) before the Mosaic provisions regulated the practice for the nation of Israel.

The tithe was an act of worship that acknowledged God's ownership of man's possessions. According to Leviticus 27:20-33, one-tenth of all the produce of the land and of all flocks and herds was to be given to the Lord. The tithes were to be given for the support of the Levites (Num. 18:21), who, unlike the other tribes, were given no land inheritance in Canaan. The Levites in turn were required to give tithes of the tithes they received to the high priest (Num. 18:26, 28).

David Chilton has called attention to the fact that in the life of Israel the Levites provided social, educational, and even medical services in addition to their strictly ecclesiastical function.[4] The implication for our present situation is that our tithing should support not only the work of the institutional church, but other Christian organizations as well that attempt to extend the lordship of Christ in the world. Independent mission organizations, Christian schools, hunger relief, pro-life groups, and many others come to mind in this regard.

A further provision concerning tithing is found in Deuteronomy 14:28,29. Every third year the tithes were to be brought to the various towns and villages and shared with the Levites, sojourners, widows, and orphans. The tithe was thus tied in the law of Moses to regular "social action" in relief of the poor. This form of welfare had the advantage of being locally administered and of bringing giver and recipient into personal contact with one another. Being administered only every third year, it did not promote the growth of a whole class of dependent people, as has been the case with many modern welfare systems.

In the New Testament, tithing is not mentioned as a specific legal obligation. Christians are, however, expected to give regularly (I Cor. 16:2) and generously (I Tim. 6:18) to the work of God. The apostle Paul, in connection with the collection for the poor in the Jerusalem church, teaches that the believer is to give cheerfully and willingly in response to God's gracious gift of salvation in Jesus Christ (II Cor. 8:8-15; 9:6-15). Generous giving is, in fact, evidence that God's grace is working in our hearts.

If the people of God of old were constrained by law to give, the people of the New Covenant are constrained by the mercies of God to show kindness and liberality. As the early Christian father Irenaeus put it, "The Jews were constrained to a regular payment of tithes; Christians, who have received liberty, assign all their possessions to the Lord, bestowing freely not the lesser portions of their property, since they have the hope of greater things."[5]

David Clowney of Westminster Theological Seminary has called attention to the fact that if American Christians faithfully tithed their personal income, some $50 billion dollars would be available for the work of the kingdom. "Think of the possible effect on world missions, on Christian relief and development projects, on refugee resettlement efforts, and on the troubled cities of this country," says Clowney.[6] A recovery and consistent practice of the biblical principle of tithing by the American church at large could have a staggering impact on our nation and the world as a whole.

Stewardship of Time, Talent, and Work

Boston Herald American columnist Ben Stein some time ago noted a Department of Labor study that cited "changing attitudes in the work place" as a cause of lagging American productivity. "In plain English," observed Stein, "too many of our workers are incompetent and lazy, products of ever more inadequate schools and a chaotic society."[7] According to reports from the auto industry, younger workers entering the industrial labor force routinely sabotage the machinery they are supposed to be running.

In recent years it seems that the "Protestant work ethic" has been disappearing from the American scene, only to emerge in Asian states such as Taiwan, Hong Kong, Japan, and Singapore, where Christianity has not yet made a significant impact. Our current economic difficulties should be seen as a challenge to the Christian community to rediscover and reassert its historic biblical understanding of the nature of work and the stewardship of time and talent. The world of work is a very critical area in modern life where Christians are called to be the salt of the earth and the light of the world.

The foundation for a biblical understanding of work is found in the "dominion mandate" of Genesis 1:28, where men and women created in the divine image are commanded to "fill the earth and subdue it; and have dominion over the fish of the sea and over the birds of the air and over every living thing that moves upon the earth." Work is certainly the means by which we "earn our daily bread" and keep our households and families functioning, but according to Genesis, work has a wider meaning. Work is the means by which we are called to *exercise dominion* for the sake of God's honor and kingdom, "subduing the earth" in our various areas of responsibility, whether it happens to be the home, the office, a business, or a factory. Since *the earth is the Lord's* (Ps. 24:1), we are to exercise stewardly dominion over it on his behalf, for the purpose of establishing God's rule and kingdom over every aspect of the creation. A Christian businessman who conducts his business as unto the Lord (cf. I Cor. 10:31) and a Christian homemaker who, like the ideal wife of Proverbs 31, manages her own household with energy and skill, are both in their own ways extending the kingdom of God in the world.

Every Christian is called to be a "prophet, priest, and king" in his or her respective area of responsibility. As "prophets," we apply the law of God to our homes and families and work; as "kings," we rule in our various spheres of activity on God's behalf; as "priests," we offer to the Lord the fruits of our labors, consecrating them unto his honor and glory. "Whatever you do"—whether baking bread or washing dishes or teaching children or running a business—"do all to the glory of God" (I Cor. 10:31).

As evangelical Christians, we are prone to concentrate on the Great Commission (Matt. 28:19,20) and to neglect the dominion mandate (Gen. 1:28). It is vital that American Evangelicals once again realize that *the Great Commission has not abrogated the dominion mandate.* We are commanded by God both to evangelize the world and to extend God's reign over every aspect of human culture. The two dimensions of Christian calling are interdependent. Without evangelism and the conversion of the human heart, lasting cultural change is virtually impossible. But without dominion activity to reclaim the culture, Christians will increasingly become isolated islands of piety in the midst of a world hostile to their values. If schools, businesses, governments, and the media are left without the leavening influence of Christian values, what the Christian attempts to build in the home and church will increasingly be eroded and destroyed by the culture at large. The dominion mandate reminds the Christian that he or she is not called simply to preserve the faith behind the walls of a spiritual ghetto, but to actively extend that faith into the world.

The Bible provides not only the framework for understanding the ultimate meaning of work, but also specific teaching on the quantity and quality of works that the believer is called to perform. "Six days you shall labor," God commands. The fourth commandment places a limitation on the number of days of work, but we also need to notice that the commandment assumes that we will be *working for six days*. God expects his people to be energetic and diligent—to set an example to the pagans in this respect. Whether our work is inside or outside the home, if we work diligently and efficiently for six days, then we will be free to devote the seventh day to the worship of God, spending quality time with our families, and to special works of ministry and service. For the homemaker, this could mean organizing the cooking on Friday and Saturday to avoid laborious cooking on Sunday. For the student, this means studying on Friday and Saturday for Monday's exam, and planning ahead to avoid a last-minute rush on the term paper. Diligence and efficiency is then rewarded with new freedom and leisure, and the Sabbath becomes the time of refreshment and renewal that God intended it to be.

In relation to working diligently for six days, Dr. Gary North advises that under normal circumstances, "salaried people should work no more than 40 hours for an employer . . . that extra 10 or 20 hours should be invested in church service or in the establishment of a family business or in getting a better education, or in community service." I may be giving 40 hours to an employer to earn income, but that other time should be invested in ways that promote family welfare and the interests of God's kingdom. "Never give away to an employer," writes North, "what you should be giving away to God, especially time."[8]

By being diligent and efficient in the home and office, we have more time to give to Christian service. The needs in this area are growing at precisely the time when the number of volunteer workers, because of economic pressures, seems to be diminishing. The number of Christian agencies, for example, prepared to "love, counsel and help unwed mothers is very small, and the ones I know of struggle to meet their modest budgets," observes David Clowney.

"The need for long-term volunteer commitment to such ministry, as well as for concerted political action, far outstrips what evangelical Christians have so far been willing to supply," he notes.[9] Diligence and efficiency in our work frees the time necessary to advance the kingdom of God in such areas.

The Bible gives specific instruction not only on the quantity of work, but also on the quality of work. Not only are we to give a "full day's work for a full day's pay"; we are to perform work that is distinguished by its *competence* and its *excellence*. In an age when poor workmanship, faulty repairs, and slipshod quality seem so common, the Christian has a real opportunity to give a testimony for the transforming power of the gospel through the quality of his or her work.

The apostle Paul reminded the converted slaves that even in the case of a non-Christian master, they were to work in "singleness of heart," pleasing God and not men. "Whatever your task, work heartily, as serving the Lord and not men" (Col. 3:22,23). Such Christian attitudes and practices in the world of work commended the gospel to a pagan world.

The life of Joseph is a striking biblical example of how competence and faithfulness in work lead to godly dominion and blessings for the culture. Whether in prison or in Pharaoh's court, Joseph distinguished himself by his competence, dependability, and insight. "Because he understood God's principles . . . and because he was able to apply them accurately to the situation in which he found himself, Joseph proved of inestimable value to every master who employed him," notes James B. Jordan in *Christian Reconstruction*. In due time Joseph was promoted to second in command over all Egypt. "The story of Joseph," comments Jordan, "tells us that the road to victory, dominion, and mastery is through service, the humble service of a slave."[10]

Christians are called to be "Josephs" in their areas of responsibility, whether in raising children or in running a business. Even a world that may not understand our religion can recognize and appreciate competence in work. God blesses those who are faithful and competent in meeting their responsibilities with greater authority and influence. By accepting the challenge to be "Josephs" in our own time, we are simultaneously fulfilling the spirit of both the dominion mandate and the Great Commission and are contributing our part to the extension of God's kingdom in the world.

Stewardship of the Future: Children

In concluding our discussions of Christian stewardship, we will briefly consider family size and the teaching of children. Neither subject is usually discussed in relation to economics and steward- ship, but both, as we shall see, can have a great impact on the economic well-being of a society. Christian decision making in these areas can influence the future shape of American life for literally generations to come.

Decisions concerning family size are a crucial aspect of our Chris- tian stewardship of the future. At this point the biblical outlook and the modern climate of thought seem to be sharply opposed to one another. The Bibie considers a large family to be a blessing: "Sons are a heritage from the Lord, the fruit of the womb a reward" (Ps. 127:3). The modern climate of opinion, on the other hand, tends to look upon a large family as a burden or even as a curse.

Environmentalists such as Paul Ehrlich consider population growth a "cancer" needing to be "cut out." If necessary, they say, the United States government should use its power "to halt the growth of American population."[11] Such perspectives assume that population growth is out of control, that it produces impoverish- ment for a society, and that "zero population growth" is a moral necessity. Such considerations will obviously affect a married couple's thinking concerning family size. But are the assumptions of the "ZPG" perspective in fact correct? An examination of the ZPG outlook will show that its basic assumptions are open to serious dispute.

In the first place, recent studies show that while population growth is still a matter for concern, it is hardly a "cancer" that is "out of control." A World Fertility Survey sponsored by the United Nations and the United States Agency for International Development found that fertility levels in the developing countries were declining at dramatic rates. According to Dr. Phyllis Piotrow, director of the Population Information Program at Johns Hopkins University, the survey showed that "there is a demographic revolution—birth rates are coming down much faster than anyone expected."[12] A study by the Population Reference Bureau concluded that "in the world as a whole, there appears to be enough land and water to meet food demands during the next half century."[13] Future threats of famine are likely to arise as much from political and social causes as from the absolute numbers of people.

Here in the United States, declining fertility rates should be viewed as a cause for concern; not rejoicing. For several years U.S. fertility rates have been below replacement levels, hovering around 1.8 children per woman. Economic writer Warren Brookes has pointed out that beginning in 1983, declining rates of American population growth will be reflected in high school graduating classes that are two to three percent smaller than the previous one, while retirement losses in the work force will be growing at six percent per year. This means that serious shortages of skilled workers are likely to show up in the mid–1980s, complicating the nation's attempts at economic recovery.[14]

Declining rates of population growth in the United States have also produced an aging population.[15] The retirement age group is growing almost four times as fast as the population as a whole. The massive problems that this development is creating for the Social Security system are now well known. The basic problem is caused by the dramatic increase in the number of beneficiaries relative to the number of younger workers paying into the system. Declining rates of population growth have only served to make the crisis more intense.

Another questionable assumption involves the relationship between population density and per capita income in a given society. It is commonly believed that high population density and high rates of population growth that can produce it are inevitably associated with poverty and low rates of economic growth. This simplistic analysis is not, however, supported by the facts. Countries such as the Netherlands, Taiwan, and Japan, which have very high population densities, are prosperous in spite of their relative lack of natural resources. The average resident of Hong Kong is better off than the average citizen of India, even though India has a lower population density and greater natural resources.

The experience of these Asian nations shows that it is not population density per se, but rather the spirit of the people and the free market that are the keys to a nation's prosperity. With enlightened government policies that promote the free market, a young and growing population can be an economic asset. "People bring not only mouths and hands into the world but also heads and brains," Professor Julian Simon of the University of Illinois has pointed out. These new people "cause technological advances by inventing, adapting, and diffusing new productive knowledge," and so contribute to the economic well-being of society.[16]

The clear implication of this discussion is that Christians should consider themselves under no obligation to limit their family sizes to replacement levels. On the contrary, Christian couples should be encouraged to have larger-than-average families. Christians, of all people, have the moral values that, being transmitted to the next generation, can provide the foundation for a just and enduring society. For all their good intentions, ZPG environmentalists are contributing to the deepening Social Security crisis. Christian parents, on the other hand, who send godly and diligent children into the world are making the most important contribution of all to the strengthening of our social and economic order—the replenishment and broadening of our base of human resources.

What values, then, should Christian parents transmit to the next generation? The first priority, of course, is the Christian faith itself. But more specifically, if the principles of the free market are rooted in biblical teachings concerning the very nature of man and society, then Christian parents should teach those principles to their children. It seems appropriate to conclude our discussion with some specific suggestions along these lines.

Dr. Gary North has stressed the importance of starting such teaching at an early age. Long before junior high the child should be

developing a clear understanding of the principles of private ownership, personal responsibility, and stewardship.

In the matter of private ownership, for example, Tommy should
not be forced to share his toy with Billy, if the toy really belongs to
Tommy. While sharing is a Christian virtue, God wants us to learn
to share *willingly:* "God loves a cheerful giver." Forced redistribution in the home misses that point and, instead, teaches children the
legitimacy of forced redistribution as practiced by the government.
A child will learn quickly enough by himself that children who never
share their toys are not very popular with their peers.

A young girl's recent letter to Ann Landers provides a vivid
example of compulsory sharing.[17]

> Dear Ann Landers:
>   My little sister is 14. We both baby-sit for extra money. . . . I
> make a lot more than she does. Mom makes us pool our money
> and divide it evenly every month. I don't think this is fair. She
> says sharing is more important than money.
>   —*Hillsdale, Mich., Complaint*
>
>   I'm all for sisterly love, but your mom is advocating Marxism.
> I favor the free enterprise system myself. People should not be
> forced to share what they earn with others who earn less, for
> whatever reason.
>   —*Ann Landers*

Encouraging the child to share with the less fortunate is certainly
biblical, but coercive sharing is another matter.

Of course, the other side of the coin of private ownership and
personal responsibility is that if Tommy loses or destroys his own
toys, then that is his problem. Rather than expecting Mommy or
Daddy to buy a new replacement, Tommy must learn to be the
steward of his own possessions, and to bear responsibility for his
own actions. Children, too, can learn to exercise dominion over
their limited areas of responsibility.

Somewhat similar considerations apply to the practice of tithing.
If the child is receiving a regular allowance, he should be encouraged—not forced—to tithe from that allowance. Rather than being
given a quarter by the parent to put into the collection plate, the

child assumes responsibility for his walk with God by deciding to give from his own allowance. The child can then "learn what sacrifice is," notes Dr. North. He learns that our personal economic decisions are to be made in the context of a life of obedience to God.

These, then, are a few ways in which the free market principles discussed in this book can be brought to bear in the lives of our own family members. As Christians we work and play and worship not merely for the present, but for the future and for coming generations. The family is one of the primary avenues through which the Christian church can contribute to a brighter future for all Americans. John Stuart Mill once said, "The family, justly constituted, would be the real school of the virtues of freedom." Christian families that are, in practice, schools for the values of Christ and the Bible are the most effective of all schools for the "virtues of freedom." Christian parents who faithfully teach their children the biblical virtues of diligence, personal responsibility, and faith in the God who controls the future make a vital contribution to the social and economic well-being of society that will be felt for generations to come.

Notes

Chapter 1

1. This description is drawn from Thomas Molnar, "Oh, Benares," *National Review*, March 20, 1981, p. 290.

2. Cited by Ronald Wallace, *Calvin's Doctrine of the Christian Life* (Grand Rapids. Eerdmans, 1961), p. 132.

3. Alfred North Whitehead *Science and the Modern World* (Cambridge: Cambridge University Press, 1926), pp. 17, 18.

4. Cited by F. J. Rutherford, *et al., The Project Physics Course* (New York: Holt, Rinehart, Winston, 1970), Unit 2, p. 76.

5. Cited in Jack B. Rogers and Donald K. McKim, *The Authority and Interpretation of the Bible* (San Francisco: Harper and Row, 1979), p. 231.

6. W. H. Gardner, ed., *Poems of Gerard Manley Hopkins* (New York: Oxford University Press, 1948), p 70.

7. George Gilder, *Wealth and Poverty* (New York: Basic Books, 1981), p. 268.

8. Ludwig Von Mises, *Human Action* (Chicago: Contemporary Books, 1966), p. 158.

9. Lord Acton, in Bergan Evans, ed., *Dictionary of Quotations* (New York: Delacorte Press, 1968), p. 547.

10. In Henry B. Dawson, ed., *The Federalist* (New York: Charles Scribner's Sons, 1890), p. 334.

11. Ibid., p. 360.

12. Gilder, *Wealth and Poverty*, p. 265.

13. Cited by Daniel Seligman, "Keeping Up," *Fortune*, March 9, 1981, p. 46.

Chapter 2

1. Robert Sabath, "The Bible and the Poor," *Post American*, February/March, 1974, p. 5.

2. Cited by Walt and Ginny Hearn, "Voluntary Poverty," *Post American*, February/March, 1974, p. 11.

3. Matthew Henry, *A Commentary on the Holy Bible*, 6 vols. (New York: Funk and Wagnalls, n.d.), 2:491.

4. Theodore W. Schultz, *Investing in People: The Economics of Population Quality* (Berkeley: University of California Press, 1981), pp. 90, 125.

5. Cited in J. Eichler, C. Brown, "Possessions," *New International Dictionary of New Testament Theology*, 3 vols. (Grand Rapids: Zondervan, 1976), 2:832 (hereafter, *NIDNTTh*).

6. Colin Brown, *NIDNTTh*, 2:838.

7. "Possessions," *NIDNTTh*, 2:832.

8. Cf. the similar statement of Coolidge, "There is an inescapable personal responsibility for the development of character, of industry, of thrift, and of self-control," in Robert A. Woods, *The Preparation of Calvin Coolidge* (Boston: Houghton Mifflin, 1924), p. 275.

9. Cited in *Parade*, June 28, 1981, p. 6.

Chapter 3

1. Cited by Charles Krauthammer, "Rich Nations, Poor Nations," *New Republic*, April 11, 1981, p. 20.

2. Cited by Jim Wallis, "Of Rich and Poor," *Post American*, February/March, 1974, p. 1.

3. Henry Hazlitt, "The Problem of Poverty," *The Freeman*, June, 1971, p. 323.

4. Ibid.

5. Ibid., p. 324.

6. *Boston Herald American*, December 21, 1979, p. A9.

7. Michael J. Boskin, "Prisoners of Bad Statistics," *Newsweek*, January 26, 1981, p. 15.

8.. Nick Eberstadt, "Hunger and Ideology," *Commentary*, July, 1981, p. 41.

9. Ibid., p. 43.

10. Louis Kraar, "Make Way for the New Japans," *Fortune*, August 10, 1981, p. 176.

11. Max Singer and Paul Bracken, "Don't Blame the U.S.," *New York Times Magazine*, November, 1976, p. 34.

12. Ibid.

13. P. T. Bauer, *Western Guilt and Third World Poverty* (Washington, D.C.: 1976), pp. 3-5.

14. James Michener, *Reader's Digest*, January, 1977, pp. 149-50.

15. Kraar, "Make Way," p. 179.

Chapter 4

1. Jeremy Rifkin, *Entropy: A New World View* (New York: Viking Press, 1980), pp. 194, 195.

2. Jim Wallis, "Of Rich and Poor," *Post American*, February/March, 1974, p. 1.

3. Dom Helder Camara, "The Fetters of Injustice," *Post American*, February/March, 1974, p. 6.

4. Ronald J. Sider, *Rich Christians in an Age of Hunger* (Downers Grove, Ill.: InterVarsity, 1977), pp. 88-95.

5. Ibid., p. 93.

6. David Chilton, *Productive Christians in an Age of Guilt Manipulators* (Tyler, Tex.: Institute for Christian Economics, 1981), p. 138.

7. J. H. Bernard, in *The Expositor's Greek New Testament*, 5 vols., ed. W. Robertson Nicoll (Grand Rapids: Eerdmans, repr. 1970), 3:88.

8. Walt and Ginny Hearn, "Voluntary Poverty," *Post American*, February/March, 1974, p. 11.

9. Gary North, *Remnant Review*, July 17, 1981, p. 2.

10. Milton and Rose Friedman, *Free to Choose* (New York: Harcourt Brace Jovanovich, 1979), p. 144.

11. George Gilder, *Wealth and Poverty* (New York: Basic Books, 1981), p. 171.

12. Ibid, p. 183.

13. Ibid., p. 184.

14. Cited by Friedman, *Free to Choose*, p. 146.

15. Daniel Seligman, "Ruling Class in Poland," *Fortune*, March 9, 1981, p. 42.

16. Mervyn Matthews, *Privilege in the Soviet Union* (Winchester, Mass.: Allen Unwin, 1978).

17. Eric Hoffer, "What America Means to Me," *Reader's Digest*, September, 1976, pp. 169-70.

126   *Your Wealth in God's World*

Chapter 5

1. Cited by Milton Friedman, "The Path We Dare Not Take," *Reader's Digest*, March, 1977, p. 113.

2. *Macon Telegraph and News*, June 28, 1981, p. 7A.

3. Quoted by Leonard Read in *The Freeman*, February, 1975, p. 75.

4. Clarence Carson, "Economy in Government," *The Freeman*, June, 1981, pp. 346ff.

5. Henry Hazlitt, "Poor Relief in Ancient Rome," *The Freeman*, April, 1971, pp. 215-19.

6. Ibid.

7. The English experience is cited from Henry Hazlitt, "The Poor Laws of England," *The Freeman*, March, 1977, pp. 137-46.

8. Arthur Ashe, "Black America Still Has a Dream," *Reader's Digest*, July, 1978, p. 85.

9. Quoted in *Newsweek*, January 26, 1981, p. 19.

10. Cf. Daniel Seligman, "Keeping Up," *Fortune*, February 23, 1981, p. 41; Walter Williams, "The Shameful Roots of Minority Unemployment," *Reader's Digest*, October, 1979, pp. 21-26.

11. Milton and Rose Friedman, *Free to Choose* (New York: Harcourt Brace Jovanovich, 1979), p. 238.

12. Ralph K. Bennett, "CETA: Eleven Billion Dollar Boondoggle," *Reader's Digest*, August, 1978, p. 72.

13. George Gilder, *Wealth and Poverty* (New York: Basic Books, 1981), p. 161.

14. Reported on NBC Nightly News, June 26, 1981.

15. Gilder, *Wealth and Poverty*, p. 159.

16. *Fortune*, June 2, 1980, p. 41.

17. Cf. Gilder, *Wealth and Poverty*, p. 111, and M. Stanton Evans, reviewer of James L. Clayton, *Does Defense Beggar Welfare?*, *National Review*, March 7, 1980, p. 308.

18. *FAC-Sheet*, Plymouth Rock Foundation, No. 31, p. 2.

19. *Reader's Digest*, April 1980, pp. 83, 84.

20. *Atlanta Constitution*, August 17, 1981, p. 6A.

21. *Reader's Digest*, April, 1980, pp. 83, 84.

22. *Macon Telegraph*, June 18, 1981, p. 1A.

23. *U.S. News and World Report*, July 20, 1981, p. 12.

24. *Reader's Digest*, August, 1979, pp. 127, 128.

25. *Reader's Digest*, September, 1980, p. 14.

26. *Reader's Digest*, December, 1976, p. 81.

27. *Macon Telegraph and News*, June 28, 1981, p. 7A.

28. Thomas Sowell, "The Uses of Government for Racial Equality," *National Review*, September 4, 1981, p. 1013.

29. Gilder, *Wealth and Poverty*, p. 71.

30. Friedman, *Free to Choose*, p. 119.

31. Gilder, *Wealth and Poverty*, p. 127.

Chapter 6

1. Cited in Arnaud C. Marts, *Philanthropy's Role in Civilization* (New York: Harper and Bros., 1953), p. v.

2. Ibid., p. xii.

3. Warren Brookes, "There Is No Better Weapon against Poverty than Capitalism," *Boston Herald American*, December 21, 1979, p. A9.

4. George Gilder, *Wealth and Poverty* (New York: Basic Books, 1981), p. 112.

5. Milton and Rose Friedman, *Free to Choose* (New York: Harcourt Brace Jovanovich, 1979), p. 37.

6. R. C. Sproul, "Robbing Hood," *Tabletalk* 5:2 (February, 1981):1.

7 Thomas Sowell, "We're Not Really 'Equal,' " in *Newsweek*, September 7, 1981, p. 13.

8. Cited in Ronald H. Nash, "The Economics of Justice: A Conservative's View," *Christianity Today*, March 23, 1979, p. 29.

9. Ibid.

10. Marts, *Philanthropy's Role*, p. 26.

11. Gerhard Uhlhorn, *The Conflict of Christianity with Heathenism* (New York: Charles Scribner's Sons, 1879), p. 191.

12. Cited in ibid., p. 204.

13. Ibid., p. 205.

14. Marts, *Philanthropy's Role*, p. 7.

15. See W. E. H. Lecky, *History of European Morals* (London: Longmans, Green, 1911), 2:85, 100, for similar comments on the influence of Christian philanthropy.

16. Robert D. Linder, "The Resurgence of Evangelical Social Concern," in David F.

Wells and John D. Woodbridge, eds., *The Evangelicals* (Nashville: Abingdon Press, 1975), p. 199.

17. Cited in Richard F. Lovelace, *Dynamics of Spiritual Life* (Downers Grove, Ill.: InterVarsity, 1979), p. 372.

18. Martin E. Marty, *Righteous Empire: The Protestant Experience in America* (New York: Dial Press, 1970), p. 94.

19. Cited in Timothy L. Smith, *Revivalism and Social Reform* (New York: Abingdon, 1957), p. 163.

20. Ibid., p. 8.

21. For a good review of evangelical social concern in the nineteenth-century urban scene see Norris Magnuson, *Salvation in the Slums: Evangelical Social Work, 1865–1920* (Metuchen, N.J.: Scarecrow Press, 1977).

22. Smith, *Revivalism*, p. 176.

23. K. L. Woodward and S. Monroe, "Colson Goes Back to Jail," *Newsweek*, September 7, 1981, p. 41.

24. Interview in *Eternity*, July–August, 1980, p. 20.

25. "Social Security, The Family and the Elderly," FAC - Sheet # 22, Plymouth Rock Foundation (P.O. Box 425, Marlborough, NH 03455).

26. Ibid.

27. Friedman, p. 106.

Chapter 7

1. Cited in *National Review*, September 4, 1981, p. 1037.

2. Cited in *The Freeman*, October, 1973, p. 625.

3. Norman Podhoretz, "The New Defenders of Capitalism," *Harvard Business Review*, March–April, 1981, p. 97.

4. Paul Johnson, in *The Freeman*, January, 1979, pp. 53.

5. *Dallas*, episode aired July 3, 1981.

6. Eugene C. Bianchi, "Capitalism and Christianity Revisited," *Christian Century*, December 6, 1972, pp. 1241-44.

7. Ibid., p. 1242.

8. Ibid., p. 1243.

9. Ibid.

10. Quoted by George M. Taber, "Capitalism: Is It Working?," *Time*, April 21, 1980, p. 45.

11. Ernest van den Haag, "Sense and Nonsense about Wealth and Poverty," *Fortune*, July 13, 1981, p. 152.

12. Cited in Taber, "Capitalism," p. 43.

13. Ibid.

14. Cited by Henry Hazlitt in *The Freeman*, March, 1973, p. 154.

15. Cited in Podhoretz, "New Defenders," p. 98.

16. Taber, "Capitalism," p. 55.

Chapter 8

1. Hedrick Smith, *The Russians* (New York: Times Books, 1976), p. 60.

2. Paul Johnson, "Has Capitalism a Future?" *The Freeman*, January, 1979, p. 48.

3. Ibid.

4. Ibid., p. 49.

5. F. A. Hayek, ed., *Capitalism and the Historians* (Chicago: University of Chicago, 1954), p. 159.

6. Ibid., p. 158 n. 26.

7. Susan I. Brown, *et al.*, *The Incredible Bread Machine* (San Diego: World Research, Inc., 1974), p. 13.

8. Lawrence W. Reed, "Witch-Hunting for Robber Barons," *The Freeman*, March, 1980, p. 169.

9. *Macon Telegraph and News*, June 17, 1981, p. 1.

10. Hans F. Sennholz, "The Great Depression," *The Freeman*, April, 1975, p. 206.

11. Milton and Rose Friedman, *Free to Choose* (New York: Harcourt Brace Jovanovich, 1979), p. 85.

12. George Taber, "Capitalism: Is It Working?" *Time*, April 21, 1980, p. 55.

13. Ibid., p. 45.

14. *Macon Telegraph and News*, September 13, 1981, p. 11a.

15. Shawn Tully, "Mapping the Second Economy," *Fortune*, June 29, 1981, p. 40.

16. Smith, *The Russians*, p. 64.

17. *Boston Globe*, March 2, 1981, p. 3.

18. *Macon Telegraph and News*, September 13, 1981, p. 14a.

19. Professor Gorden Fee, personal communication, 1981.

20. John W. Cooper, "The Cuban Revolution," *Christianity and Crisis*, July 21, 1980, p. 203.

21. *Time*, April 21, 1980, p. 53.

22. David Reed, "Singapore: Jewel of Prosperity," *Reader's Digest*, November, 1979, p. 226.

23. Michael Novak, *The Smith Kline Forum for a Healthier American Society*, vol. 3, no. 6, September, 1981.

24. Taber, "Capitalism," p. 55.

Chapter 9

1. Barry Commoner, *The Closing Circle* (New York: Knopf, 1971), p. 255.

2. Jeremy Rifkin with Ted Howard, *The Emerging Order: God in the Age of Scarcity* (New York: Putnam, 1979), p. x.

3. Lynn White, Jr., "The Historical Roots of Our Ecologic Crisis," *Science* 155 (March 10, 1967):1203-7.

4. "Moses adds, that the custody of the garden was given in charge to Adam, to show that we possess the things which God has committed to our hands, on the condition, that being content with a frugal and moderate use of them, we should take care of what shall remain." John Calvin, *Commentaries on the First Book of Moses Called Genesis*, trans. John King, 19 vols. (Grand Rapids: Eerdmans, 1948), 1:125.

5. Francis Schaeffer, *Pollution and the Death of Man* (Wheaton, Ill.: Tyndale House, 1970), p. 70.

6. Henlee H. Barnette, *The Church and the Ecological Crisis* (Grand Rapids: Eerdmans, 1972), p. 79.

7. Ibid., p. 80.

8. John Maddox, *The Doomsday Syndrome* (New York: McGraw-Hill, 1972), p. 140.

9. Paul Johnson, *The Enemies of Society* (New York: Atheneum, 1977), pp. 91, 92.

10. Maddox, *Doomsday Syndrome*, p. 131.

11. Ibid., p. 137.

12. *World Research Ink*, November/December, 1979, p. 17.

13. Ibid.

14. *Newsweek*, August 31, 1981, p. 68.

15. J. L. Simon, "Resources, Population, Environment: An Oversupply of False Bad News," *Science* 208:4451 (June 27, 1980):1431-37.

16. *Los Angeles Times*, August 21, 1978, in *World Research Ink*, November/December, 1979, p. 18.

17. James A. Weber, "Energy Ethics: A Positive Response," *The Freeman*, April, 1981, p. 199.

18. Simon, "Resources," p. 1436.

19. *Newsday*, August 28, 1981, p. 62.

20. *Wall Street Journal*, June 23, 1981, p. 53.

21. James Miller, "Bonanza! America Strikes Gas," *Reader's Digest*, April, 1981, pp. 65-71.

22. *Wall Street Journal*, September 14, 1977, p. 22.

23. Ibid.

24. William J. Baumol and Wallace E. Oates, *Economics, Environmental Policy and the Quality of Life* (Englewood Cliffs, N.J.: Prentice Hall, 1979), p. 107.

25. *Newsweek*, May 18, 1981, p. 33.

26. *Boston Globe*, May 12, 1981, p. 23.

27. *Business Week*, July 6, 1981, pp. 48-52, 56.

28. Ibid.

29. *Mother Earth News*, July/August, 1981, p. 124.

30. Simon, "Resources," p. 1436.

31 Peter Berger, "Ethics and the Present Class Struggle," *Worldview*, April 1978, p. 10.

32. Cited in Simon, "Resources," p. 1437.

Chapter 10

1. George Gilder, *Wealth and Property* (New York: Basic Books, 1981), p. 74.

2. Gary North, "Ownership, Responsibility, and the Child," *The Freeman*, September, 1971, pp. 515-21.

3. Luke 16:10.

4. David Chilton, *Productive Christians in an Age of Guilt Manipulation* (Tyler, Tex.: Institute for Christian Economics, 1981), p.44.

5. Cited in Gerhard Uhlhorn, *The Conflict of Christianity with Heathenism* (New York: Scribner's, 1888), p. 199.

6. David W. Clowney, in *The Bulletin of Westminster Theological Seminary*, Spring, 1981, p. 5.

7. Ben Stein, *Boston Herald American*, November 1, 1979, op-ed page.

8. Gary North, "The Calling," *Christian Reconstruction*, March/April, 1981, p. 2.

9. Clowney, *The Bulletin*, p. 5.

10. James B. Jordan, "Joseph's Job," *Christian Reconstruction*, May/June, 1981, p. 1.

11. Paul R. Ehrlich, *et al.*, *Human Ecology: Problems and Solutions* (San Francisco: W. H. Freeman, 1973), p. 278.

12. Cited in *New York Times*, August 10, 1979, p. A8.

13. Cited in *U.S. News and World Report*, November 26, 1979, p. 94.

14. Warren Brooks, *Boston Herald American*, January 16, 1979, op-ed page; see also William P. Butz, *et al.*, *Demographic Challenges in America's Future* (Santa Monica: Rand Corporation, 1982), pp. 23-25.

15. See "The Graying of America," *Newsweek*, February 28, 1977, pp. 50ff., and William C. Freund, "The Looming Impact of Population Changes," *Wall Street Journal*, April 16, 1982, p. 34.

16. Julian L. Simon, "Resources, Population, Environment: An Oversupply of False Bad News," *Science* 208 (June 17, 1980):1434. See also the major study on population by the same author, *The Ultimate Resource* (Princeton: Princeton University Press, 1981).

17. *Boston Globe*, July 15, 1981, p. 51.

For Further Reading

Biblical Economics Today. Institute for Christian Economics, P.O. Box 6116, Tyler, Tex. 75711. Published six times a year by Gary North; free market, limited government, hard money perspective.

The Freeman. Foundation for Economic Education, Irvington-on-Hudson, New York 10533. A monthly publication; articles and reviews supporting a free market perspective.

Milton and Rose Friedman, *Free to Choose.* New York: Harcourt Brace Jovanovich, 1979.

George Gilder, *Wealth and Poverty.* New York: Basic Books, 1981. Shows how capitalism is rooted in faith, family, and work.

Henry Hazlitt, *Economics in One Lesson.* New York: Crown Pubs., Inc., 1979. A concise and classic discussion from a conservative perspective.

Harold Lindsell, *Free Enterprise: A Judeo-Christian Defense.* Wheaton, Ill.: Tyndale House, 1982. Lindsell is a former editor of *Christianity Today.*

Ludwig von Mises, *Human Action: A Treatise on Economics.* Third edition. Chicago: Contemporary Books, 1966. A major work from the "Austrian" school of economics; originally published in 1949.

Gary North, *The Dominion Covenant*. Tyler, Tex.: Institute for Christian Economics, 1982. See especially chapter 4 for an incisive criticism of nontheistic theories of economic value. Available from Institute for Christian Economics, P.O. Box 8000, Tyler, Tex. 75711.

Michael Novak, *The Spirit of Democratic Capitalism*. New York: Simon and Schuster, 1982. A spirited defense of the morality of the free enterprise system.

Tom Rose, *Economics: Principles and Policy from a Christian Perspective*. Milford, Mich.: Mott Media, 1977. A useful textbook. Available from Mott Media, 1000 E. Huron, Milford, Mich. 48042.

Hans F. Sennholz, *Age of Inflation*. Belmont, Mass.: Western Islands, 1979. Incisive analysis of the causes of inflation by a professor of economics at Grove City College, Grove City, Penn. Available from Western Islands, 395 Concord Avenue, Belmont, Mass. 02178.